Finding the Small Business that Fits

Marc Schneider

for my children - Emma, Benjamin & Zachary

"This represents everything I know on this topic to this point."

Acknowledgements:

I would like to thank my wife Stefanie and the many friends & family that contributed the lessons and examples for this book.

I also want to thank my friends & family that took the time to edit my draft manuscript. I would also like to thank my professional editors Jamie Parker and Bethany McKay.

Lastly, I would like to thank Milos Komadina from *Belgrade, Serbia* for the cover artwork, and Tamta Kondzharia from *Zaporizhzhia, Ukraine* for the chapter graphics.

Copyright 2024 Marc Schneider, Orbit Industries NJ, LLC

Contents

Introduction...	1
Chapter 1 - Why Write This Book?...	5
Chapter 2 - My Business Experience..	9
Lawn Mowing / Snow Shoveling...............................	9
The New York News Page...	12
Stinger Stylus..	21
Medical Vending Machines.......................................	29
Tidbit...	33
Photo Screw Art..	38
Spine Ice...	42
Chapter 3 - Money...	47
Accounting..	48
Investment and Working Capital...............................	48
Payment...	49
Recurring vs. One-Time Income...............................	51
Seasonal Income...	51
Franchises...	52
Lawsuits..	52
Personal Guarantees...	54
Chapter 4 - Time..	57
Chapter 5 - Skills...	61
Chapter 6 - Assets...	65
Chapter 7 - Business Type...	69
Service-Based Businesses...	70
Product-Based Businesses..	72
Hybrid Businesses..	74
Complex vs. Simple Businesses...............................	75
Industry...	76
Margin & Turnover...	77
Rental Businesses...	78
Chapter 8 - Location..	81
Chapter 9 - Customers...	85
Chapter 10 - Partners / Employees...	89
Chapter 11 - Marketing..	95
Chapter 12 - Risks...	99
Profit Margin Risk..	100
Sticky Brand Loyal Customers.................................	101
Competition Risk..	102
Regulation and Zoning Risks....................................	103
Recession and Liquidity Risks..................................	104
Other Risks to Consider..	105
Chapter 13 - Future..	109
Conclusion...	113

Introduction

Home from college for the summer, my friend Scott and I needed money to support our taste for cheap beer and lousy food from the local diner. After seeing flyers for University Painters, a group of college kids who started a painting company, we decided to start University Driveway Sealers. We thought sealing blacktop driveways in the summer would be a simple business to start, market, and earn some easy money. We surmised it would take little effort to print flyers and then stuff mailboxes in the neighborhoods with large houses, but only buy sealer and brushes after making a sale. We figured rich people would be an easy mark for our "college-trained" driveway service. They had long driveways, and more importantly, they had plenty of money. So, we steamed ahead and made a flyer on a word processor and went to the local copy shop. We rushed out excited to make money and walked all day in the 95-degree heat filling mailboxes with our flyer. Then we waited for calls. And waited.

After a week or so, we gave up on our silly business and went to the mall. When we got home, my mom said someone had called about wanting his driveway sealed. She had told our potential customer that we were wonderful boys and would do a great job. My mom basically became our receptionist and head of sales. She had made our first sale. We rushed over to a very large house to meet the homeowner and give our first estimate. We rang the doorbell and anxiously looked at one another. Scott whispered, "You know what to say?" The door opened and a portly unshaven man in his robe asked us what we wanted. We replied, "We are from University Driveway Sealers, here to give you an estimate." He asked us about our experience and we told him we had done many driveways and were very busy, but we would fit him in the very next day. He asked for our price, and Scott looked at me. I paused, scratched my chin as if pondering, then said "$100." The homeowner said he usually pays $75 to the pros and I replied immediately, "Okay, how about $65?" My superior negotiation skills worked and we confirmed our first sale! As we turned the corner in my dad's 1976 Buick, Scott and I high-fived one another. Scott said, "You know how to seal a driveway, right?" I replied, "No, but how hard could it be?"

    The next morning, we drove over to the local hardware store to buy our supplies. Reading the back of the 5-gallon jug of driveway sealer, we realized we did not measure the driveway, and therefore did not know the square footage. We had no idea how many jugs to buy. So, we guessed and bought two jugs and two large squeegee brushes. Total cost: just over $45! Scott looked at me surprised and I said, "Well I guess we underbid the job." We drove over to the house, unloaded the jugs, and read the directions. We realized we had no way to stir the asphalt sealer, nor did we have proper shoes or tarps.

    After a short brainstorming session, we agreed on Scott's idea to pour the contents of the jug on the middle of the driveway and use the squeegees to mix it while spreading. This was a bad idea. A very bad idea. The black liquid part in the mix quickly ran in a stream down the driveway as we both gave chase with our squeegee brooms. We stepped in the tar sealer and made footprints on the sidewalk. Some parts dried quickly in the sun and other parts were wet and thick. We made a mess. We did eventually finish the job, but the homeowner was not very happy with the results. We did not ask him for any referrals and were in a rush to leave. Surprisingly, he paid us our $65! We sealed only one driveway that summer and once again relied on our parents to support us.

We made a lot of mistakes in our first small business attempt, but looking back on the experience, I feel we learned a lot. Our first goal was to make money during our free time in the summer, but we soon realized we were missing the key ingredient of a service-based business: we had no skill. Skill is the result of experience and training of which we had none. We were lucky that our mistakes in this first simple venture did not cost us much time or money. In today's world, setting up a new small business that doesn't fit one's skill set will surely cost time and money. It is good to learn from your mistakes, better to learn from others' mistakes, and best to not make mistakes in the first place. This book breaks down important attributes of various example businesses. My goal is to teach the reader how to assess their specific personal skills, assets, and desires to evaluate a small business opportunity before taking the leap. The goal is to be self-introspective and honest in finding the best venture that fits you. The "fit" is paramount to your success; that is, the success of your business and your enjoyment in running it.

Chapter 1 - Why Write This Book?

Why did I decide to write this book? Throughout my life, I tried to start, started and failed, and started and succeeded in multiple businesses. I have many friends and family members who have done the same, and I really enjoy speaking with them about their experiences. Recently, I started jotting down the attributes of a business I would like to be involved in based on my and others' experiences. More importantly, I started thinking about how I want to spend my time at my current age and what I am actually qualified to do. Other questions I asked myself were: "Will this venture make money?" "Is it worth my time?" "Can my children take this business over in the future and will they even want to?"

I remember when I was in high school, the guidance department had each student fill out a personality/skills assessment questionnaire to suggest a college major and a career path. At a mere 18 years old, I answered personality and aptitude questions for about 30 minutes. The results proclaimed that I should become a bookkeeper. I thought that was just silly, but now years later, I run a successful US bond trading operation where I am not just the head trader but also head accountant/comptroller and risk manager. So in effect, I am a glorified "bookkeeper." I wondered if there existed a questionnaire assessment for what business to start based on individual attributes and not just to match a college major and career path. I could not find any tool that provided an analysis of a sole proprietor's capabilities, interests, and resources to match them to a business that fits. With that in mind, I created a spreadsheet with multiple categories of assessment for me to look at possible companies to buy or start. This spreadsheet list morphed into the outline for this book.

    My career has been centered around working on Wall Street. I attended the University of Virginia McIntire School of Commerce and graduated with an undergraduate degree in finance. I went straight to work at Salomon Brothers, a large bond trading firm featured in the book *Liars Poker*. I completed the firm's CFO Apprenticeship training program, which qualified me to work in the middle office, a division directly supporting the revenue-producing trading desks. Interacting with the traders and assembling their daily profit and loss statements made me aspire to be one of them. After consulting with the head trader, it was strongly recommended that I get a Master's in Business Administration (MBA). So, I applied and was accepted to the Columbia Business School, and after two years and about $100k in tuition, I earned a graduate degree in finance. Right back into another Wall Street training program at a firm called Kidder Peabody, I was basically out of work before the training ended. Kidder was embroiled in a $350 million trading scandal and General Electric sold the firm to Paine Webber. The head of the sales division at our firm called a meeting of all the trainees on December 23rd and told us he would be running the sales desk at

Paine Webber. He then followed that seemingly positive announcement with the fact that we were all being laid off...Merry Christmas! We each received two weeks of severance pay. This was my first taste of working on Wall Street and corporate America, and being laid off for things completely out of my control.

After three months of going to the gym, getting certified in scuba diving, and watching the OJ Simpson trial, characterized as the "trial of the century" back in 1994, I landed on my feet. Multiple resume mailings, calls, and several interviews later, I finally was offered a job at Smith Barney, another big Wall Street firm. With no family to support and no large expenses, this process was not too stressful for me, but always stuck in the back of my mind. I always wanted to run my own company and not be at the mercy of forces beyond my control. I was very fortunate to have no student loans—thanks, Dad!

Since that experience, I have had several other large bank jobs and worked in London for a bit until I finally decided to embark on managing a proprietary bond trading operation, which I currently run today. I am the managing partner along with 20 other partners, each trading our own capital in one large account, trading securities in the US Treasury market. My primary role is to manage the trading risk and all of the trading systems. My other roles include daily profit and loss statements, paying company bills, doing all accounting/tax work, and hiring/firing traders. I also manage our relationships with interdealer brokers and our clearing house. Secondary duties include lease negotiations, air conditioner servicing, desktop tech support, and a multitude of small and meaningless, yet necessary tasks. All of these daily duties are done concurrently with my own personal trading. Neither my time spent at the large Wall Street banks nor my Columbia MBA adequately prepared or trained me to succeed in this role.

I started pondering what personal attributes and experiences contributed to my current success in running a bond trading firm. I thought back to all the companies that I worked for and the tuition dollars my father spent, and came to this conclusion: there is no substitute for actual experience. Reading this book, taking classes, and spending your life working for other people does not replace spending *your* time and *your* money while forgoing a salaried profession to learn and succeed at running your own business.

...A small note on what this book is not:

This book is not intended to be critical or demeaning to any type of business, or type of employee or customer. There are many successful companies that run counter to my experiences and opinion of an ideal venture. My anecdotes and experiences are only particular to my attributes and my life path. For example, I would shy away from a business requiring a significant fixed overhead or one that needs lots of working capital to operate. Nor would I prefer an enterprise where the owner spends inordinate amounts of time collecting outstanding accounts receivables. However, there are many very successful businesses with owners who are very happy with these attributes.

Further, this book is not meant to advise the reader on legal structures and methods of financing, nor to give legal or tax advice. Many experts have written extensively on these topics. Lastly, this book is not intended to go into detailed analysis on any one topic, but rather it is a general overview to allow the reader to be thoughtful and reflective.

Chapter 2 - My Business Experience

My first successful endeavor was in the seventh grade. I had the good fortune of taking over my brother's lawn-mowing business as he went off to college. This was a proven and easy operation to run with no costs. My brother had paved the way with our dad in using the family lawn mower to cut our neighbors' lawns. Further, we used our dad's gas and he paid for maintenance, which included new mower wheels when needed. We did put the wheels on, which was the least we could do in exchange for his financial generosity. I learned that this business required very minimal sales and marketing. I received my initial jobs from my brother and neighborhood family friends. Once in a while, a new passerby would stop me while mowing and ask me to give an estimate for their lawn. It was a pretty easy and relatively cost-free service business to market.

Further, my only requirement was to mow the grass once a week according to my own schedule and then knock on the door and get paid. I had no costs, no marketing, no schedule, and no accounts receivables. This first venture may have been my best, other than the fact it required a benefactor to cover my costs and required a lot of manual labor in the hot summer sun. Another major pitfall with this undertaking was that it had no barriers to entry. Professionals with commercial mowers and a truck could easily underbid me with the strategy of upselling homeowners for lucrative landscaping services. I learned that lawn mowing was really only a conduit for professional landscapers to sell far more profitable services such as paver patios, expensive tree plantings, and rock and mulch for flower beds. This was a good first business that taught me some valuable lessons.

    My second venture of shoveling driveways in the winter was a natural successor to mowing lawns in the summer. I already had many of the customers and it was an easy sell. However, the work was irregular as it was obviously weather-dependent. And when it snowed and I had a day off from school, I much preferred going sledding, building forts, and having snowball fights with my friends. Shoveling driveways was once again a manual chore in the bitter cold, which was not very fun. However, the pay was good and there wasn't much competition in my neighborhood. The seasonality and weather dependency of lawn mowing and shoveling snow, along with my distaste for manual labor in the heat and bitter cold, have stayed with me as I assessed future endeavors.

Lessons Learned:

Sealing Driveways:
- Get experience/training on how to price and do the work.
- Know your market—which neighborhoods have money.
- Don't expect immediate success and don't give up.
- Build referrals.

Lawn Mowing:
- No accounts receivable.
- Easy to keep customers, hard to convert new ones.
- Manual labor in the hot sun is tough.

Snow Removal:
- Weather-dependent businesses are not great.
- Do a job no one else wants to do.
- Manual labor in the cold is tough.

Reader Notes:

"All the News that Fits on One Page"

THE NEW YORK NEWS PAGE.

At Columbia Business School, I took an entrepreneurship class where the students were required to create a formal business plan for a new small company. Looking back, I think the process of learning and writing a business plan was invaluable. I strongly recommend all entrepreneurs write a detailed business plan for any venture they are considering buying or starting. My plan was for a start-up called *The New York News Page*. This was a free handout in the New York City subways that contained the daily news on one sheet of paper. It would be funded by advertising on the perimeter of the page. The logic was that New York City had flyer distributors on many street corners handing out advertisements that no one wanted. Combining the news with these local ads would incentivize taking the paper. Not only did I write the business plan, but my two friends and I actually started the business (one was my friend Scott from our failed *University Driveway Sealers* college venture).

We had no sales experience and no skills to write news or create graphic design layouts for news print. Further, we found out that handing out flyers or any material other than religious literature in the subways during the NYC rush hour would require permits from the Metropolitan Transit Authority (MTA). We really had no idea where to start, so we each kicked in a hundred dollars and applied for permits with the MTA. We made some prototypes of our newspaper on our computers on an 8 ½-by-11-inch page with empty blocks on the edges of the page saying "*Your Ad Here*". We set up a phone-answering service that gave us a telephone number and a prerecorded message that we spent hours recording and re-recording. We finally got the perfect outgoing message to greet the multitude of potential clients looking to advertise on our free news page. We then had a local print shop make us each a box of business cards with the title "Owner and Founder" under our names. We thought this would give us clout and prestige when we were selling ads. We dressed in collared shirts and khaki pants, placed our prototype of *The New York News Page* in leather folios, and took to the city streets. We started in the Grand Central area of midtown Manhattan. This was our first foray into soliciting and cold-calling.

We walked for hours in the summer heat into local stores asking to speak with owners. The standard answer from front desk personnel was that the owner was not in that store or unavailable to see us. We would leave our business cards and a sample news page for the owner to review and call us about placing an ad. We soon realized that this was not a good method to sell ads in our new and unproven one-page newspaper. After a couple of days, my friend Scott's parents insisted he focus on his law school studies and he dropped out of the business. So, my other friend and I persevered and continued to try and sell ads. Our first big break came from a gym near Grand Central.

We met the receptionist and gave our normal sales pitch. Miraculously the owner of the gym came out and invited us back into his office. He was a white-haired man who engendered a wise grandfather figure as he inquired about our backgrounds. To our surprise, his son had gone to Tufts, a small university in Medford, Massachusetts, and graduated a couple of years before my partner. This was the luck we needed at this point in our fledgling business. We spoke for an hour or so about our endeavor and were complimented on our ingenuity and entrepreneurship. The gym owner signed a contract for a large ad in our paper for four weeks at a total contract price of $1,200! He loved the idea of us handing out his ad with the news in the subways in midtown NYC close to his gym. We shook hands and left with smiles. As we turned the street corner, we jumped up and down. Our first huge sale and now we could move forward. We collected no upfront money. We were sure we would get paid by a college friend's father. We were wrong.

  We spent a lot of time creating the proof for our large gym ad, as the gym owner assured us that once it was approved, we would receive payment. We continued to sell other very small ads and were hopeful of setting our launch date. We stopped by the gym to get the ad approved and the receptionist took our proof into the back. After several minutes she returned and said the ad was approved to run by the owner. We asked about payment on the contract, which clearly stated that "all advertising was to be paid prior to publication." The receptionist disappeared into the back once again. After several minutes she returned and said that the bookkeeper was out that day and we would need to return another day for payment. There were no alarm bells yet, but we were discouraged as we needed the funds to pay for printing costs and the hourly workers to hand out our news page. We returned the very next day and got a similar story from the receptionist. We waited a day, and then returned for our $1200 check and were told the owner was not available to see us. My brother who had recently passed the law bar exam glanced at the contract and said we had nothing to worry about. The contract was clear, the law was on our side, and we should get paid. So, we went ahead and hired staff to hand out the news page in four subway stations, had shirts and hats screen-printed with our logo, and lined up a large printer to run 10,000 two-sided copies of our daily news page.

  The two of us used our own funds plus those collected from the small ads to launch the business. We would write the short news stories at night and include late-night final sports scores from the West Coast, which we later found that our readers really liked. Larger newspapers could not wait for games to end and had to go to press, leaving early morning commuters without the final game scores (remember, there was no internet or smartphones).

Each night, we would insert the newsprint into our prepared proof with the ads and a crossword puzzle. Late at night Sunday through Thursday, one of us would need to hand-deliver the proof to the printer so the copies would be ready to be picked up at 6 a.m. the following morning. The next morning we would meet our distributors at the printer and give them their location assignments and stacks of news pages. Later in the morning rush hour, we would go into the subways and check on the distributors. This was a really time-consuming and tough business to start and operate, especially while in graduate school.

Our launch was well-received in the NYC subways. It was a real morale boost for us to get on the midtown subway shuttle between Times Square and Grand Central and see most of the riders standing in the car reading our one-page newspaper. We even got featured on a local television news channel with comments from some of our readers. Selling ads became a bit easier as we refined our sales pitch and actually had circulation. Some of our solicitations were met with local business owners telling us they had seen our paper in the subways, proving very helpful in closing a sale. Our nightly process became more efficient as we found an API news service where we could cut and paste the small opening paragraphs from the top stories of the day. We also hired a car service to pick up the nightly proof and deliver it to the printer. But all was not so easy.

We ran our $1,200 gym ad for the full month while stopping by each week to ask for payment. Finally, the owner came out and invited us into his office. He had a friend in his office whom he was trying to impress with his macho tough talk. He reprimanded us saying that our paper was garbage and he had obtained no new gym members from his advertisement. Further, he doubted we even handed out the 10,000 copies per day per the contract. He said he was paying us nothing for the ad, and abruptly threw us out of his office. When we protested saying we had a signed contract and were not leaving without payment, he threatened to call the police. We left and never received payment. I wanted to file a lawsuit, but my partner disagreed and said it would cost too much, and we needed to focus on building our business. It was a $1,200 lesson that was well-learned and never forgotten.

As we continued to sell ads and make our new operation more efficient and profitable, we decided to increase the size of our news page to 11 inches by 17 inches to allow for some more news from our API feed, but more importantly, more paying advertisements. We added a column from my then-girlfriend, now wife, called "Dear Stefanie" modeled after the "Dear Abby" column. Stefanie who was in NYU graduate school at the time earning her master's in social work, would write a problem that a supposed reader wrote in, then would write her suggestions. No one really wrote into our fledgling newspaper with a real issue, but the made-up problems and solutions were entertaining and had a following from our readers. We had some fun with our newspaper but made many mistakes. We received a threatening legal letter from a law firm representing the *Daily News*, a large tabloid newspaper in New York. They were unhappy with our tagline displayed at the top of our news page which read "All the Daily News that Fits on One Page". It was surprising that *The New York Times* wasn't upset with us for playing off their slogan "All the News That's Fit to Print". The lawyers argued that readers were under the impression our one-page newspaper was affiliated somehow with the *Daily News* and we had to modify our tagline.

We also made mistakes sometimes with the news. In a rush to meet our friends at a bar on a Thursday night, we labeled an article with the headline "Major Earthquake in India Kills Thousands". The API article had the correct location in Indonesia, but we typed the headline in error. Luckily while at the bar, we saw a news story on a television and realized our mistake. We ran back to our apartment and fixed the headline and got the correction to the printer before it ran. These were small errors and misjudgments that are part of all start-ups and should be expected. However, bigger problems were on the horizon.

Selling advertisements was our only source of revenue. Both my partner and I were in graduate MBA programs and were juggling multiple roles. The stress of keeping the business funded and operating began to erode our friendship, as each of us overvalued our contribution of labor, sacrifice, and ad sales. One advertiser who I will never forget was a sole law practitioner. We had sold him a small advertisement in our news page to market his legal services, mostly estate planning and the preparation of wills. My partner and I both sold the initial ad together. One of us would stop by his office when we were in the area to discuss how his ad was performing and try to resell the lawyer on another week. He was young and just starting. He had a co-op office suite with one receptionist and communal office equipment/conference room. We would always meet in the conference room as his office was small and unimpressive. We had the same pitch: brand recognition and repetition from his ad would get him new clients We sold him on multiple occasions, one week at a time every time we had space. One of us would go by and cut him a "great deal," and he would always fall prey to sacrificing his hard-earned money in the hopes of building his business. All he was doing was helping to float our doomed news page.

I knew our business was failing, and the daily grind was becoming too onerous. With pressure from my parents, it was time for me to accept a job in finance at a large brokerage firm and better utilize my expensive Columbia education. My partner wanted to keep the venture going with the hope of a big break from a large ad sale that could be right around the corner. Hope and luck are two things not to count on in building a business. Toward the end, my partner came back one day and told me he had sold our lawyer a four-week ad at a huge discount. I was upset and felt bad for the lawyer. Even though our job in sales was to make promises and sell, I knew our newspaper would never deliver for him. I felt sure no one would call an estate lawyer from a free newspaper handed out in the subways, and I was not confident we would continue to operate for another four weeks.

The proverbial "nail in the coffin" for our one-page newspaper came during these frustrating and financially tense final weeks. We had multiple locations in the subways in midtown NYC and periodically I would check on the distribution. I went to our Port Authority location one morning to find our distributor leaning on the wall staring into space. If we had smartphones in 1992, he would have been staring at his phone. I knew that location well as I had personally handed out the news page several times and knew how many pages were taken per hour from 7 to 9 am. It was 8 am and my young distributor was done with his work. He was surprised to see me and immediately blurted out that he had run out of papers. He was so naive, and his laziness was so obvious, that when I looked in the nearby garbage can and saw all of our news pages, he quickly said, "Those were misprinted." I reached in and pulled out hundreds of pages that were perfectly fine, and immediately fired him on the spot. The multitude of expletives that I used in my anger went unnoticed by the commuters and probably passed off as just another day in the NYC subway.

That evening when my partner checked the company voicemail, he looked stunned. He paused, then said I needed to listen to the message. Apparently, our recently fired distributor left a message that he needed his job and relied on the money. If he didn't get it back, he would show up in the subway and shoot me. I was shocked that he would leave such a message, then a little scared, then realized he might be dumb enough to actually do it. So, after some deep thought and discussion, we did the smart thing. We called him and offered him his job back, but kindly asked him not to throw the newspapers into the trash can and not to shoot either of us. He agreed. We shuttered the news page the very next week.

Looking back, I learned more from starting and running this operation than I did in any of the graduate MBA classes at Columbia. I learned how to create a business from scratch by teaching myself design software, soliciting ad sales, collecting money, and managing employees. The hardest part was working with my friend and partner when our interests were no longer aligned. In both a successful business and a failing one, the partners either claim more of the credit or place blame. Another lesson I learned was that even though I really disliked soliciting, all businesses required selling and collecting money. I decided I would never again sell a product or service that I truly did not believe in. It always felt wrong to sell ads to the estate lawyer just to fill our empty spots each week. In the end, we did return his money for the last couple of weeks that his advertisement did not run.

Lessons Learned:

- Get some portion of payment upfront.
- Have partners to share responsibilities, time, ideas, and various skills.
- Hire good people, especially ones who don't want to murder you.
- Think about how much time and when you can commit to work.
- Outsource tasks that you can do that are not worth your time.
- Think about the costs of working with friends and family.
- Avoid lawsuits.
- Believe in what you are selling.

Reader Notes:

In 1998, I was working as a proprietary bond trader and had some free time to work on a new venture. After my experience with the one-page newspaper, I decided that a product-focused business would fit my current lifestyle and time constraints better than a service-based venture. The Internet was exploding and websites were becoming the new way of marketing and selling. Handheld personal data assistants (PDAs) were also becoming extremely popular, most notably the Palm Pilot. These were small pocket-based electronics that the user could input their Rolodex of contacts along with their calendar, task lists, calculator, and other simplistic games. The PDA was the predecessor of the smartphone. Palm created a touchscreen interface with a very intuitive short-hand letter-drawing input called Graffiti. One could quickly input letters into the device using quick swipe patterns on the screen with the tip of your finger. Users also tapped on icons on the screen to navigate the various menus and applications. Palm provided a small plastic stick called a stylus that was used like a pen for these inputs and was stored in a receptacle tube on the device. I noticed many people lost this stylus and resorted to using their fingertips, causing the screen to become smudged and dirty. As a guitar player, I thought of the idea of a finger-pick stylus containing an adjustable ring to fit various finger sizes with a stylus tip at the end. The product would be called Stinger, as it resembled a bee stinger.

I drew multiple prototypes during the design phase and settled on an adjustable strap that would go around the user's finger. The adjustment would be made with small pegs on one side of the strap fitted into holes on the opposite strap. This method was used as the sizing mechanism on many of the baseball hats I wore in my youth. I decided to pursue a patent to protect my innovation. My friend Adam was designing websites and his father, still living across the street from my parents, was a patent attorney. After several meetings and patent searches, I moved forward and filed both a design and utility patent for the "Adjustable Finger Stylus." My legal fees at the "friends and family" rate were $10,000. Adam began work on designing the website and I offered him 10 percent of the business for his efforts. The next step was to find manufacturing, which I preferred to do in the United States. I assumed a simple two-part injection mold and some prototypes should not be too expensive. Once again, I was wrong.

After multiple calls, I found a local injection manufacturer who was willing to meet with a new inventor, as most plastic companies only dealt with large customers. They had a great design staff who helped fine-tune the measurements, the method of snapping the adjustment bands, and the sampling of the correct material to mold the malleable strap and the firm stylus tip in one simple plastic product. They did have minimum molding requirements, and along with the single cavity mold (i.e., each close and open of the machine yielded one product), I had to make another $10,000 investment. It was stressful spending more than $20,000 on a product patent and prototypes with no proof of concept nor actual demand. Additionally, I had no method of marketing as I was unsure of how and where to advertise. I had no experience in retail product distribution and had a lot to learn, but luckily I had the time and capital to invest.

When the product design and correct plastic mix were dialed in, the patents were filed and the design and production of packing was completed. Luckily, I was pretty good with Adobe PageMaker and Illustrator software from my Newspage days and was able to do the patent drawings and package layouts myself. This skill saved me time and money.

The next step was sales. I manufactured the minimum required 5,000 pieces and decided to sell them in 3-packs. I priced the 3-pack at $7.95 including shipping, and my friend built the website and shopping cart functionality to allow customers to click and buy via the Internet. Today we take this concept for granted, but in 1998, this type of transaction was very new. In terms of marketing and internet searching, Facebook, Instagram, and Google did not exist and Web-based advertising mediums were not an option. Print ads in papers and magazines were expensive and did not target our niche audience of Palm Pilot owners. I decided that the PC Expo convention being held in New York City at the Jacob Javits Center was the way to launch the product. Renting a small booth on the basement floor underneath all of the huge exhibitors was shockingly expensive at $3,000 for a two-and-a-half-day show. In addition, the booth needed to look professional, so I spent more money on background signage, table/stools, and brochures. The goal was to give away thousands of free samples to spark interest and awareness in the consumer electronics market. I needed some luck in this product launch to recoup my $25,000 investment, and the Palm Pilot booth upstairs turned out to be our golden goose.

When the expo started, my friend Adam helped me in doing product demos and handing out lots of free samples. I decided to walk upstairs to the big booths and network with some of the larger company exhibitors. I showed the Stinger to the personnel at the Palm Pilot booth and they loved it! All of the staff in the booth wanted one so I ran downstairs and retrieved a bunch to give to them. Later in the day I walked by the Palm booth and saw all of the Palm demonstrations being done with the Stinger stylus. This was a real morale boost and made all the effort and time worth it. We finished the show having handing out all the samples, packed our materials, and left not sure what the next step would be in terms of marketing. Then, I was contacted by someone from Palm. That is when the real luck hit!

Palm Pilot was a relatively new product and the leader in the PDA space. When consumers bought their product, they had a warranty registration card that included the owner's name, address, and, most importantly, email address. In 1998, email was relatively new and the concept of spam and junk mail did not exist. Palm executives decided to use their treasure trove of newly acquired email addresses to start a Palm newsletter to market new applications and peripheral products to their registrants. These were targeted Palm owners who represented a golden marketing opportunity. I was told they wanted a single advertiser on the Palm newsletter and it was to be the Stinger finger stylus! This was terrific news, and the best part was they would run our advertisement for FREE! Adam and I quickly made a nice photo-based ad of the Stinger suitable for email per their specifications and submitted it. Our contact at Palm gave us little details on when the mass email would drop and to how many users, as they were still assembling their content. A couple of weeks later, our contact told us the newsletter email would drop that weekend and would be sent to more than 1,000,000 Palm owners. We were very excited but had little idea what was coming.

My first thought was we were going to get a lot of recognition and press. My second thought was that I hoped the website would hold up and process the orders. Adam assured me the site and servers were resilient and would handle the order flow. So, we patiently waited and kept checking our email for the Palm newsletter. Finally, it was emailed out and the website lit up. Adam built a summary frontend for us to monitor the website page views and order flow. We were astounded with the results. During that weekend, we had more than 50,000 page views of our website and received about 9,000 orders. That equated to about $75,000 in sales revenue! I started to panic, as we had very little inventory and no system to package, address, and mail 9,000 orders. And the orders kept coming in.

 Our first step was to set up an automated email that said our demand was large and orders may be delayed several weeks. Some people sent in cancellations, but most customers were patient. That Monday, I called our New Jersey plastic injection manufacturer and asked how long to cut a second cavity in our mold. The mold was capable of handling two imprints, but I only cut one side to save money and allow for design modifications. Now the main concern was production time and per unit cost versus the cost of the mold work. The manufacturer was able to get the mold work cut in less than a week. And now the per unit cost was reduced in half. In the injection molding process for small items, the primary driver of cost is machine time. Now, each time the mold closed and opened, two Stingers came out. The additional material cost was negligible. I also asked the manufacturer for help with packaging and they referred me to a product fulfillment company. This company could take the loose products and place three Stingers in the package, fold over our hand tag, and staple the finished product. This seems like a simple process, but when multiplied by 10,000, it becomes very time-consuming. We purchased a Pitney Bowes postage machine and Adam created address labels that contained both our return address, the recipient's address, and a simple numerical code to identify the order information (i.e., color/quantity/envelope size/postage amount). We then ordered boxes of mailing envelopes in various sizes to be delivered to my home and set up multiple tables in the basement for an assembly line. My wife, friends, and their spouses came over at various times to stick address labels, affix postage, and later stuff/seal envelopes when we received products. The whole ordeal was fun, stressful, and full of paper cuts and favors owed to friends.

The big error looking back at this experience was thinking that this stroke of luck in marketing would launch the product and sales would continue to grow. I ordered quite a bit of extra inventory with the anticipation that orders would keep coming. They did not. Orders from the newsletter surged for several days then dropped off dramatically. Once Palm owners ordered our product, that was it. They didn't need more than three, and referrals to friends failed to go viral. Palm did allow us to advertise in a future newsletter to even more users and they charged $1,000 for the ad. This was still a great deal, but the explosive sales did not follow as this obviously was a one-time event. We did get some press in *The New York Times* technology section, *US News*, and several other publications, but orders from our website never really flowed in. The only option was to try and get the Stinger into retail outlets, which proved very difficult.

I contacted several office product retail chains and Walmart. We were lucky when Staples headquarters returned our call and requested samples, and our product media kit. Over time with several follow-ups, they agreed to sell the product at eleven key stores throughout the country as a test. This seemed like a great opportunity, but the devil was in the details. We would need to provide each store with 2,000 packages with no payment upfront. So effectively, we were providing 22,000 3-packs of Stingers to Staples on consignment. If the products sold in a specific time period, they would pay us and order more product. If it did not sell, we were responsible for the return shipping of the unsold items back to our warehouse. This did not seem like a very good risk and I declined the offer from Staples.

The main complaints with the Stinger adjustable finger stylus was where to store it when not in use. Many users lost the Stinger, just as they had lost their Palm stylus and once again resorted to using their fingertip. They did not reorder our product, which was telling. We did not see repeat orders. Further decline in our sales emanated from the popularity of the Blackberry handheld, which included a small keyboard that eliminated the need for a stylus. But Blackberry eventually lost popularity to the iPhone and the many other handheld smartphones with their incredible LCD touch screens that required a finger to interact with the conductive screen. Our plastic stylus would not work. The Stinger had run its course, and the website and business were shuttered. The business was profitable and provided valuable lessons in product design, manufacturing, marketing, and understanding of the retail selling process. The one aspect that was most appealing about this product-based business was there were no accounts receivable. Selling a product via the Web required no collections of money. A customer bought the product and paid for it, which was a very attractive attribute in assessing future endeavors.

Lessons Learned:

- Product prototypes and patents are expensive.
- Pick a business that utilizes your knowledge base and skills.
- Marketing a new product is expensive.
- Be prepared for success.
- Don't expect luck in marketing to occur more than once or at all.
- If no repeat orders in a product-based business, there is a problem.

Reader Notes:

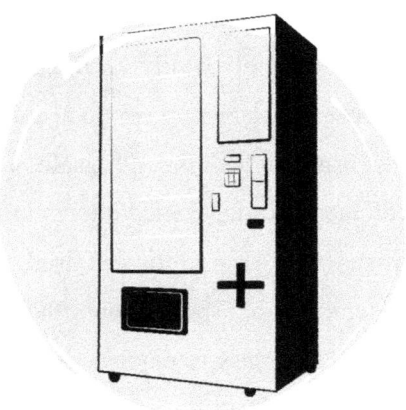

As the Stinger stylus business was winding down, my wife and I attended a franchise expo at the Jacob Javits Center in New York City. Walking around as a patron versus an exhibitor gave me a different perspective. I could see many vendors trying to sell franchises with varying degrees of professionalism. Some of the franchise exhibitors on the lower floor seemed desperate in their sales pitch. From the view as a prospective customer, most seemed like their business was a failure and the only money-making venture was to sell franchises. On the top floor, the large, well-known franchises had terrific professional booths with numerous well-dressed staff members, presenting their business and chatting with prospects. These household-named franchises required huge upfront capital outlays and full-time hard work, but they promised success.

My wife and I stumbled upon a medical vending machine franchise booth on the lower floor, which looked interesting. After a short conversation about the benefits of vending Advil, Tylenol, and other single-packet, brand-name medicines from a small wall-mounted vending device, we were told they were running a special, but "only for today." If we purchased three machines, we could save $5,000. The "normal" price was $5,000 per machine and they held exclusive distribution of these patented high quality vending devices. I liked the concept of vending a product, as there were no accounts receivables, only money collection from the lock box post-sale.

Further, medicine vending seemed interesting as the machine required no electricity as was required for soft drink and candy vending, and the medicines generally didn't spoil. Lastly, the machines took up very little space and should be easy to place. The franchise salesman offered little help in placing the machines other than to provide a short operating manual and advice in their paperwork. We would pay no franchise fee but would be required to purchase the medicine and future devices from the franchiser on an ongoing basis. After meeting some other pushy franchise salespeople, my wife and I left the expo with some business ideas that needed further research.

The Internet was becoming very useful as a tool for research and I was able to locate the manufacturer of this particular exclusive high-end medical vending equipment. I spoke with the manufacturer's salesperson, and they told me they had no exclusive sales contracts with any franchises, and I could buy directly from them at $1,200 per machine with no minimum purchase requirement. It seemed odd that the franchise salesman had lied to me (*sarcasm*), and was attempting to make $3,800 profit per machine! I guess *caveat emptor*, "Let the buyer beware," always applies.

I created some basic marketing material and called several local manufacturers. I thought installing a vending device for medicine on a factory floor would perform better than in an office environment, as the shop workers had no desk to store bottles of medicine. This strategy proved successful after two different manufacturers contacted me about installing medicine devices. I hadn't bought any machines yet, but did set up two different sales plans. In the first plan, I would buy and install the equipment, and vend medicine at $0.50 per packet. The second plan had the factory buying the machine from me at $2,000, and I would set the vend price at $0.25 per packet, then bill them monthly for the other $0.25 per vend. Some manufacturers had health departments tasked with handing out over-the-counter medications, and they wanted to end that practice. They preferred the lower vend price but wanted to own the equipment installed on their wall. This model was the better of the two, but both models worked well. The difficulty came in placing machines.

    I was able to install several devices and the business was profitable, but not lucrative. The vending business requires regular visits to the machine to refill, collect the coins, and clear any jams. The "high quality" vending apparatus tended to jam often and required maintenance, and the machine only had about $25 worth of coins to be collected. The time spent driving and gaining access to the factory floor, fixing and refilling, and then driving home was several hours. This business quickly illustrated an insignificantly profitable enterprise. Luckily I had not purchased $10,000 worth of devices, but rather did my research and saved a lot of money. I ended up selling the installed machines to the factories that had not already owned them and gave them the keys and instructions for refilling. I was able to cleanly exit this business, learning some lessons about the value of my time and luckily making a small profit.

Lessons Learned:

- Be careful buying into a franchise; do your research.
- Vending seems great but is not lucrative without owning multiple machines in various locations.
- Placing machines safe from vandalism in high traffic locations is difficult.

Reader Notes:

When our children were very young, my wife and I would occasionally take them to fast-food restaurants. One chain gave a small prize with the children's meal that my young son Ben really enjoyed. It was a small voice recorder with two buttons to record a simple message and then play it back. One day, I recorded a comforting message that ended with me saying goodnight on the toy as my wife and I left to attend a wedding. Upon our return the next day, our babysitter told me that my son had repeatedly played my recorded message over and over before bed. This experience gave me the idea for a stuffed plush toy that contained a recordable chip that could store multiple short messages. I sketched a cute owl, as the wise connotation would be a fitting stuffed animal to convey short "tidbits" of knowledge in the form of recorded messages from various family members. There would be two messages in each of five categories for a total of ten chambers for loved ones and friends to leave messages and memorable quotes. I presumed there would be a market for young children who had traveling parents, long-distance grandparents, or siblings and friends away at camp or college. This new product-based business would be called Tidbit and I had my friend Adam once again build a website. It was called TidbitToy.com.

Another friend ran a business that had contacts in China for manufacturing products, so I used this resource to make a prototype plush toy. This part was easy, but creating the electronic voice box with ten buttons to store messages that the user could record, play, and re-record was a bit difficult and more costly. After multiple attempts and shipping time from China to the US, I had a working prototype. The minimum order was 500 pieces, and the cost landed in the United States was about $20 per unit. Once again, I had a $10,000 upfront cost much like the Stinger stylus start-up a decade earlier. Also, I was once again faced with the challenge of launching a new product: marketing and sales. Even though I thought this product was novel, cute, and filled a need, getting the word out would be difficult.

Shipping the Tidbit Toys to the United States from abroad required safety testing, correct labeling, and customs forms. After researching these items and navigating through the China to US shipping container process, the 500 Tidbits arrived at the Port of Newark, New Jersey. I then booked a local trucking company to have the shipping container of plush toys transported to my home. After several months of logistics and costs, the 42 large boxes finally arrived, each with 12 Tidbits individually packaged in plastic. As I began to open the boxes and inspect each item, I soon realized that a Chinese quality inspector in China would have been most useful. More than 50 percent of the Tidbits were sewn poorly, had broken zippers, and had voice box recorders that did not function. This was quite disheartening. Luckily, my friend's contact in China was honorable and asked me to send photos of the poor-quality merchandise. He coordinated the pickup of about half of the Tidbit Toys and paid for the shipment back to China. These were to be returned to the manufacturer and either repaired or replaced at no cost to me. I was very lucky to have only lost time, and not money, in my first foray into Chinese manufacturing.

During the manufacturing process, I was creating packaging, product hangtags, and marketing brochures. I investigated the upcoming toy fair, once again at the Jacob Javits Center in New York City, as one option to launch, but I was late to the exhibitor registration process. So, I decided to attend as a guest to look for competing products and creative marketing ideas. In speaking with large toy exhibitors and small individual inventors with single products, I decided the Tidbit should be sold in boutique mom-and-pop toy stores instead of large retailers like Walmart and ToysRUs. I also decided to submit my product to specialty outlets such as Sharper Image, Brookstone, SkyMall, Hallmark, and QVC. These companies had online product submission forms for small toy inventors and seemed easier to make contact. Some even requested product samples and submission contracts. I also searched the Internet for local toy and hobby shops in the tri-state area and created a database and mailing labels. I sent out my Tidbit marketing brochures, business cards, and pricing information to all of these regional small toy stores. Then I waited. And waited. No return calls or interest came in for my Tidbit toy owl.

My next step was to use the solicitation skills learned during the *New York News Page* experience. I walked into several local toy and hobby stores and asked to speak with the owner. Most of the owners were hard to get a meeting with, but one owner seemed promising. I met with a woman who was extremely complimentary of the idea and really liked Tidbit. When I asked her to put it on her shelves, the tone of the meeting changed drastically. She said her store was not taking any new products and was very busy. She wished me luck and went into the back office. I was stunned and about to leave, but decided that I deserved a reason. So, I asked the cashier to ask the owner to come back, as I had one last question. She returned and looked angry. I told her that I had spent a lot of money and time on the Tidbit owl and wondered why she would not help me sell them in her store, especially when she liked the product. The owner replied that she found it was too difficult to work with small inventors in terms of shipping, product returns due to defects, customer service, etc. She was only interested in dealing with large manufacturers via distributors. That was the end of our discussion.

    The marketing experience of the Tidbit Toy was very discouraging. My last hope was to generate some buzz. My wife would give the Tidbit as a gift to all of the children's birthday parties that my three young children attended in town. I had hoped this would generate some grass roots demand for the product. After several years and multiple encouraging compliments from friends about how their children loved the Tidbit, the sales via the website were zero. The market had spoken and I had about 350 Tidbits stored in my attic and no more kids in town who didn't already have a Tidbit. Every time I go into my attic, I see all the owls staring as if they are mocking me. I did donate several hundred to a New York hospital pediatric cancer ward, which was the silver lining that came from the Tidbit experience. However, the education I obtained in the retail toy business was quite expensive.

Lessons Learned:

- Manufacturing in Asia is cheaper, but shipping logistics and quality control are difficult.
- Selling a single product to retail without a distributor is very tough.
- Attend industry shows to assess your market and competitors.
- The retail toy industry is extremely hard.
- Inventors focus on great products and fail in the marketing process.

Reader Notes:

Friends of ours who collect artwork asked me to view a piece they had recently acquired by an artist named Christian Faur. He would take thousands of handmade colored crayons and assemble them into a mosaic. When viewed from several feet, the individual crayons, each representing a pixel, begin to blend, allowing the viewer to see the subject in the piece. This struck me as a very innovative and unique art medium. In my friend's artwork, I noticed that a tip on one of the crayons was broken, as someone had unwittingly touched the fragile piece. In jest, I suggested to my friend that I could make that type of art, but my work would not be fragile. My friend mockingly replied that I could never replicate such an intricate and expensive piece of art. Answering the challenge, I investigated various media and settled on metal sheetrock screws. I figured they could be painted in various shades and I could replicate a photo similar to what Christian Faur had done in crayons, but be far less fragile.

After many hours of working on the computer learning to break a photo down into pixels using Excel and Photoshop to create color codes, I had a paper formula for creating a photo in screws. My next step was to use a high volume low pressure (HVLP) spray gun, typically used to paint automobiles, and spray thousands of screws in various numbered gradients from white to black. My artwork was to be black and white as opposed to the color crayon mosaics created by Faur. After tinkering with the size, grayscale shade gradients, and photo layout, I was ready to build a screw art piece of John Lennon with more than 4,000 screws measuring 2 x 2 feet. Enduring several weeks of slow progress, the piece was completed. I was happy with the end result and showed the piece to the friend who had initially challenged me. He was quite impressed and commissioned me to make portraits of both of his daughters in screws. These pieces of personalized artwork hang in their home today.

    To streamline my process, I contracted with a commercial deck screw company to paint and bake the enamel screws in the multiple gray shades for my work. This made my effort far more efficient but still tedious. Each piece would take about 25 hours to complete from design inception to completion. I received requests from other friends who saw the artwork and wanted personalized pieces and portraits of their favorite musicians, a recently lost parent, or a famous person. Since my first portrait of John Lennon, I have made fifteen portraits and sold ten up to $1,500 a piece depending on the artwork and size.

    In terms of marketing PhotoScrewArt, I did not have much success. I had one piece requested by a friend to be placed in his coffee shop, which I thought would garner some publicity, but it received none. I entered a New York City street art fair for which I made a display, mobile cart, and brochures. The entire day in the sun talking about my artwork was fun but produced no publicity and no sales. I also sent emails to many art galleries with images of my work and links to my website and Facebook page. Lastly, I created a mailing list of high-end interior decorators in the tri-state area and sent my PhotoScrewArt brochure with a cover letter. My hope was they may suggest purchasing one of my unique pieces for their client's interior decor. I received only one call from a woman asking if I was the one who had sent the brochure for the artwork. I was immediately excited that my marketing worked! Upon acknowledging that I was the artist, she rudely scolded me, and said to stop sending her junk mail and take her off any future lists. I had only sent her one brochure but nonetheless, the interaction and failed marketing endeavor was quite disheartening.

    The genesis of a successful business is a topic I think about often. Many people turn an enjoyable hobby in which they possess a natural skill into a profitable business. My venture, PhotoScrewArt.com, was very much a hobby that turned into a small and profitable business. I was really interested in this meticulous and creative art medium and realized that I have a very task-oriented personality. I enjoy the process and progress that is evident as the artwork grows to completion, much like a jigsaw puzzle. However, I realized that my hourly pay rate was quite low after material costs, time spent discussing a portrait, designing the computer layout, and screwing more than 4,000 painted screws. An individual artist's work is not simple to replicate or hire employees to expand into a large business. I deduced that PhotoScrewArt.com was truly a compensated hobby and not a business.

Lessons Learned:

- Once again, marketing a unique idea is very hard.
- Before spending time and money, try to assess whether your idea is a hobby or a profitable business.
- What is the value of your time?

Reader Notes:

    Since 2001, I have suffered from lower back pain. I recall awkwardly leaning over my infant daughter's crib to place her inside gently. My focus was not to disturb her slumber as I knew that would require a repeat of the 20-minute process to get her back to sleep. While bent over the crib, I felt a small explosion in my lower back followed by immense debilitating pain that brought me to the carpet. This was the beginning of over two decades of lower back pain, including spinal disc surgery in 2014. Rehab therapy using ice packs, heating pads, stretching, and core exercises have been the norm, but most of my pain was alleviated using a rolled towel as lumbar support with a gel ice pack. My twin high-school-age sons noticed my method of pain relief and they came up with the idea for a lumbar support ice pack that stays frozen for longer than the standard 20 minutes.

    Drawing on my experience with past product-based businesses, together with my sons we decided to turn the idea into a new product. They created product design sketches and, with my help, initiated a design patent. From the sketches, we were able to pay $200 to have professional patent figures drawn by a freelance patent artist and began the arduous task of filing a design patent via the very secure US Patent and Trademark Office (USPTO) website. These types of patents normally take more than 18 months to hear back, so that was the first step. We opted not to spend the time and money on a utility patent, as it would require a patent attorney and a more than $10,000 outlay. Next, we started testing various shipping gel ice packs, foam ice blocks, and bead-style pellet ice packs. We ordered multiple swatches from hiking material websites, hoping to find the best outer shell fabric that would be waterproof and durable. After much trial and error, we chose a shell material and gel insert for the lumbar support ice pack. The next step proved difficult, as contract sewing vendors really do not want to deal with individuals and are even less willing to speak with teenage entrepreneurs. My sons needed help in making the calls and setting up prototype sample requests. After changing the shape, size, and zipper quality, we finally had a workable prototype and a reasonable small order price quote. The next step would be funding and marketing, which led them to Kickstarter.

Kickstarter is a product launch website that allows backers to fund a project for future rewards in the pre-production stage. If the project fails to meet the funding goal within the stipulated timeline, no funding or rewards are made. After much discussion and research, we set the funding goal at $3,600. This would be enough to cover the design patent drawings and filing costs, the prototype samples, and the first small production run. Before moving forward, the product needed a name, a logo, a short marketing video, and a decision on retail pricing. Bringing a product to life on Kickstarter is an arduous task but was very rewarding in the lessons learned during the process for my sons. The product was named Spine Ice and would be their first entrepreneurial endeavor. We took the time and relatively small cost to register the name Spine Ice and the product logo on the USPTO website.

Using the prototypes and the various design process photos, my sons made a short 2-minute video for Kickstarter. They explained the product details and how it stays frozen for up to 5 hours. The material quality and long-lasting freeze time would be the key benefits to people suffering from lower back pain and needing to sit on the lumbar icepack for long periods. The Kickstarter was launched with a 60-day time frame to meet the $3,600 funding goal. My sons, wife, and I publicized the Kickstarter project via our social media, asked friends and family for support, and created both Facebook and Instagram pages to help in the marketing effort. We also learned about Facebook paid advertising and tried various small marketing campaigns. The Facebook ads were able to target directly toward specific age groups and those who expressed interest in back pain, therapy, and exercise. We spent about $65 per day on Facebook ads and refined the target age group over about a week. The result was multiple clicks to the Kickstarter page and video but almost no conversions into funds pledged to the project. The only real successful funding was obtained from friends, family members, and coworkers. However, the boys did get a spike in interest after some free publicity.

After submitting the boys' lumbar support ice back story to several newspapers and local television programs, we were contacted by News Channel 12. For their local broadcast human interest segment, they sent a cameraman to our house to interview the boys about Spine Ice. A short clip of the boys being interviewed with a demo of the Spine Ice product played on the air multiple times over two days and we saw the backers grow on Kickstarter. Obtaining free publicity of this type is very important for a new business.

At the end of the Kickstarter campaign, my sons' Spine Ice project achieved 112 backers with $4,467 in pledges, which allowed the project to come to market. The next step was ordering the embroidered Spine Ice shells and the gel insert packs in bulk to fulfill the Kickstarter rewards. My daughter Emma used her graphic design background to create the product instructions inserts and package labels. We ordered shipping boxes and created an assembly line in the basement to fulfill the orders. In determining the shipping, we found that the product's weight and size made it quite expensive to ship across the country at $15 for only a $20 item, Though the US Postal and UPS shipping rates were only about $9 to ship within the East Coast. The shipping costs of this relatively inexpensive product led us to research selling and using the fulfillment systems of Amazon.

After more than a year, Spine Ice achieved great customer reviews on Amazon and was acclaimed the Amazon Choice award for ice packs. However, we do not obtain more than a handful of sales per week. I did have high hopes for my sons' invention to not only help others suffering from daily back pain but to actually make them some profits in this small one-product line business on Amazon. I personally use the prototype daily and firmly believe in the value and innovative nature of Spine Ice, yet it is not a very profitable business.

Lessons Learned:

- Marketing on Amazon and Facebook is targeted but expensive.
- Free publicity in newspapers or local television human interest stories are worthwhile.
- One great product is rarely a business.

Reader Notes:

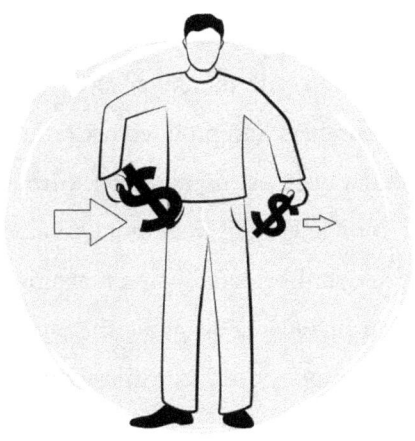

Chapter 3 - Money

The primary purpose of starting a business is to make more money than you spend running the operation. It seems like an obvious statement, but many entrepreneurs lose sight of this when embarking on a new business. Being a sole practitioner dentist, a lawyer, or owning a restaurant all require a focus on money to run your day-to-day operation. A dentist still needs to pay for office space and staff while also paying insurance, marketing, and utility bills, just like a restaurant owner. Unlike a restaurant owner, a dentist needs to collect money from insurance companies and collect accounts receivables from patients, whereas a restaurant owner generally is paid immediately. Regardless of the actual product or service, if you are not an employee, you are a business owner. As the owner, you must understand basic accounting, cash flow, working capital, and the use of credit, or your business is destined for failure. This chapter will explore the various aspects of money related to starting and operating a successful business.

Accounting

Most people express an initial distaste for accounting and proclaim they are "not good with numbers" or say they will hire an accountant to run the numbers and produce tax returns. I cannot emphasize enough that a business owner must learn accounting basics and have a working knowledge of Excel or a Quicken type financial program. One must be detail-oriented when managing their bank checkbook and general finances. Following the numbers and knowing where you are spending money are the primary drivers of success. An owner must know true costs versus revenues to understand the profitability of a business. Whether a product or service-based business, the devil is in the details. To make prudent business decisions, a business owner needs the data and the ability to analyze the figures. My suggestion would be to take a basic accounting class and a financial literacy course at a local community college if these skills are lacking. Further, a basic Excel course would be highly recommended before starting or buying a new business.

Investment and Working Capital

How much capital do you have to invest in your new venture? What is the source of this capital, and if more is needed, can these funds be obtained? What will the cost be for initial capital and future working capital needs? These are questions any entrepreneur must ask before buying or starting a new business. In terms of initial capital outlay, the same type of business can be accomplished with varying degrees of initial investment. For example, buying a car wash requires a huge capital outlay versus starting a mobile detailing company. Both are in the same automobile cleaning service industry but require vastly different amounts of initial capital.

Most prudent business owners line up sources of capital and keep cash on the sidelines to support their business, as many unknown and sudden events require funds. Being conservative and prepared with sources of money prevents panic and hasty expensive decisions when the unexpected occurs. Unfortunately, most banks will not set up a line of credit *after* an emergency occurs. This type of funding needs to be set up far in advance when times are good.

"Crawl, walk, run" is my strongly recommended mantra when starting any type of enterprise. Be conservative in initial outlays for commercial space, hiring employees, manufacturing or buying inventory, or spending on marketing. I generally dissuade the new entrepreneur from the statement "Go big or go home." A new business is like an infant and generally needs to be nurtured and grow slowly while the owner navigates the many facets and learns from mistakes. For example, the risk of having to move locations after signing a lease for space that is too small after a business grows is far less onerous than being saddled with a huge rent expense for space that is far too large. Well-planned and conservative capital investment, in general, is the key to building a successful business.

Payment

An often overlooked but very important aspect of any business is how and when your business collects payment. In the best case, a business sells its goods or service and is paid at the time of sale. Restaurants and retail stores tend to fit this form of payment as patrons come in, eat and pay or purchase a product, and then leave. There are no invoices to send and no accounts receivables to collect. This is a terrific aspect of these types of businesses. In the worst type of payment scenario, a business spends inordinate amounts of time and possibly legal fees in trying to collect overdue bills. This time drain and legal cost are a complete distraction from the goal of building a business.

Most businesses have to invoice and offer terms to customers for payment. Clients are offered terms such as "net 30" or "net 60" where the customer is asked to pay in 30 or 60 days after receiving an invoice. A friend of mine who is a lawyer and operates his own practice spends a lot of time asking for payment, and in many cases, he has to offer discounts on the final bill to collect. This uncomfortable conversation with your client is awkward, yet unavoidable. In some instances, he has refused to attend a court date unless a payment was made. Another friend who operates a Web design/hosting business has threatened nonpaying clients with shutting down their site until payment is made. This delicate balancing act of payment versus maintaining a positive client relationship is always a challenge.

Credit cards and other types of electronic payment are convenient for customers, but cost the merchant anywhere from 1 to 4 percent of the total transaction, sometimes with additional fees. Credit card payments also come with the risk of charge-backs, where the customer disputes the charge with their bank at a later date, long after the original transaction. These credit card charge-backs inevitably cost the merchant more time and money.

Cash payment has many obvious advantages, but most retailers are moving away from cash. The main benefit of instant payment is no collection, but many owners avoid paying taxes on that sales revenue, which I highly frown upon due to ethical issues and risk of tax audits. Keeping unreported cash off the revenue side of the books also hurts the owner's future valuation in efforts to sell the business. Cash businesses require on premise safes/protection, and have the high risk of slippage by employees along with danger of armed theft. Many business are moving towards only credit cards and/or use of cash app platforms such as Venmo, Zelle, and Paypal. These phone based apps are efficient and safe, but tend to have varying fee structures which require analysis by the business owner.

Lastly, many businesses make use of factoring of accounts receivables. In factoring, the vendor sells unpaid invoices to outside collection companies at various discount rates depending on the credit quality of the invoiced customer. Merchants tend to get 80 percent on average in a factoring transaction but receive their payment immediately. This 20 percent ends up being a cost to the business but is sometimes necessary when working capital and cash flow are tight.

Recurring vs. One-Time Income

A somewhat more recent trend in business is to create a recurring income from clients. I have noticed this more frequently with regard to software and streaming services. Microsoft and Adobe, in the past, sold their software and would only obtain more income in the future when the customer bought a new personal computer (PC). Now these companies all have moved to a recurring subscription model with monthly billing. Many offer customers upgrades and cloud storage, but for the most part, the customer is paying quite a bit more over time for software versus a one-time purchase. Most customers who want these software programs or streaming services like Netflix have no choice, as there is only the monthly recurring plan.

As the business owner, the recurring income model is valuable versus a one-time sale. The owner can more efficiently run their business when they know they will be receiving a certain revenue each month from ongoing customer billing. For example, a home improvement company that installs new windows or new roofing shingles only tends to get a one-time sale. Homeowners buy these items when needed but will not need them again for 20 years. These businesses have to continually spend on marketing and rely on customer referrals to generate the next sale. Whereas a home alarm installer like ADT makes an initial sale, it maintains recurring income from the monthly home monitoring service and bills the customer in perpetuity. As you look at a possible business to buy or start, it is always good to think about recurring income as it reduces the constant stress from income swings and making new sales.

Seasonal Income

Businesses that operate during certain seasons of the year face challenges in terms of cash flow. For example, a landscaper who earns a living doing yard maintenance and installing patios needs to plan for idle time during winter months. Many landscapers continue to pay valuable employees while they are idle in order to retain them. They can do snow removal, but that revenue is sporadic as it is obviously reliant on the winter weather. In evaluating a business, remember to weigh consistent recurring income more positively in your assessment rather than weather-related sporadic cash flow.

Franchises

When assessing the purchase of a franchise, a business owner really needs to analyze what they are paying for compared to what they get. Large franchises offer brand recognition, national advertising, training, and advice for building the business. In most cases, financing from banks and obtaining a commercial lease are more easily attained. The franchise owner pays large upfront fees and must kick back a share of revenues to corporate, along with paying their respective share of national ads. They are subject to corporate standards and controls, as most large franchises have stringent rules on store appearance, hours of operation, what can and cannot be sold, and product pricing restrictions. Smaller franchises offer more flexibility, but in most cases, the costs the owner pays for the franchise and ongoing revenue-sharing are too onerous. A shrewd business owner could run the business without a franchise in most cases. Speaking with other franchise owners in other locations is a must in the due diligence process for a prospective franchise investment.

Lawsuits

In most lawsuits, the only winners are the lawyers. Litigation always costs money and time, and is a major distraction from your core business. Unfortunately, lawsuits are inevitable in most businesses. Emotion and "right versus wrong" must be weighed against both the monetary costs of a lawsuit and the subjective "distraction" costs. In my experience and in speaking with many friends who run successful businesses, lawsuits are always negative experiences.

Lawsuits can emanate from many different sources in a business. Lawsuits between partners over ownership interests, retail location customer accidents, nonpayment litigation, rental property evictions, and return of security deposits are some of the more prevalent examples. I have heard of expensive and lengthy litigation related to noncompete clauses and lawyers recruiting undocumented immigrant employees to sue their employers, along with unsafe work environments and worker discrimination lawsuits.

I will never forget the experience of a friend who owns a landscaping company. He was hired to construct and install a large, multi-level marble patio by a homeowner. The total cost was $75,000 and was to be paid in thirds: one-third upon contract, one-third during construction, and the last third upon completion. The homeowner paid the first and second thirds, and never complained or raised a concern about the quality of the marble nor the design or workmanship during construction. Only after the completion of this several-month project did the owner complain and refuse to make the last payment of $25,000. Litigation, depositions, expert testimony from suppliers, and photos were presented in court, and the legal costs were astronomical. In the end, my landscaper friend prevailed, but legal and time expenses would have been better served if he had forgone the last $25,000 payment or negotiated a lower final payment to end the dispute early.

Personal Guarantees

Most new business ventures require capital and credit. Taking a loan from a bank to purchase a business, inventory/equipment/vehicles, or signing a commercial lease require new business owners to sign personally to guarantee the business's payments. In terms of risk, the lender needs to protect their loan as most start-ups tend to fail in the first year, and therefore banks and landlords require personal assets to back the loan or lease. In terms of risk for the entrepreneur, no matter how much confidence one has in their new venture, it is always prudent to spend time thinking about the possible outcomes when signing personally. Your family, home, and future are put at risk when being asked to sign personally to guarantee a business.

There are ways to limit the scope of a personal guarantee, and all options should be fully vetted before signing. For example, some assets can be excluded, such as your home or retirement accounts. Your spouse can possibly be excluded from a personal guarantee. If there are multiple partners, the guarantee can be structured not to cover more than 100 percent of the business when adding each partner's personal guarantee. An entrepreneur can also look at other methods of financing along with higher interest rate loans without personal guarantees. The concept of "betting the ranch" should not be taken lightly, and all options for financing and loans should be researched. I strongly recommend consulting with an attorney before signing a personal guarantee for any aspect of a new enterprise.

Chapter 4 - Time

Time is possibly your most scarce resource other than money, and should be thought about before embarking on a new venture. When you think about your time, don't only focus on *when* you want to work on your business but on *how* you want to spend your time. I have told my children as they thought about college majors and future careers to research what a day in the life for a particular career entails, which also applies to an entrepreneur. Do you want to spend your day in an office cubicle or work outdoors? Do you want to spend your day in a suit working in a professional environment or in casual attire in a more relaxed atmosphere? Is constant automobile and airplane travel with hotel stays an attribute that you enjoy or despise? If dealing with customers, do you want to spend time with people at their happiest moments, such as a wedding caterer or photographer, or at their worst moments, as a funeral director or divorce attorney?

In addition to writing a detailed business plan that lays out a blueprint and financial projections for your venture, an entrepreneur needs to assess their free time and make sure they can allocate the necessary resources to their fledgling business. People start most ventures while they have full-time jobs, during college, or are caregivers. Very few highly motivated people starting a new business drop their entire lives and spend all their time on a new venture. Time allocation and splitting tasks if there are multiple founding partners are very important and need to be part of your business plan. All new businesses require immense amounts of time, especially in the start-up phase, as some items just take a long time to complete. I recall waiting in an empty office all day for the Internet installation tech to arrive and get our lines set up for our computer network servers. It was a complete waste of a day, but our business was dead in the water without it. Many imperative business start-up tasks just take time, so plan and prepare so as not to be stressed and frustrated.

A business owner also needs to think about when they want to work. It seems like a simple statement, but this is quite important to your family life. For example, can your business operate when most other people are working from 9 to 5, Monday through Friday, and children are in school? Or is your business primarily a weekend operation or an evening operation? A restaurant or catering business mostly operates in the evenings and on weekends when people spend their leisure time. Bar owners need to work late nights, whereas bagel and donut shops operate early mornings until noon. A retail store needs to be open most days including weekends, versus an online product-based business that can work and create shipments anytime. As a business matures, an owner can hire supervisors and employees to run the business but don't plan on that luxury for quite some time as a new owner. Choose a startup that has a time requirement that fits your lifestyle.

Chapter 5 - Skills

Many people run businesses with a product or service that they know little about and often have no skill in that particular industry. However, in my experience and in speaking with many successful entrepreneurs, the business owner needs to be trained and skilled, and have an in-depth understanding of their product or service. They should have a true interest in the industry, as well. I recall my friend's father worked in Israel in the commercial construction industry operating heavy equipment. He came to the United States and started his own water drainage and sewerage construction company. Not only did he build this company over 25 years, but he frequently visited job sites where large diggers and backhoes were excavating and laying huge concrete water pipes in the ground. My friend told me that his father would often arrive at the job site, stop the work, and climb into the ditch to check the grading. He would kick the operator out of the machine and take the helm of the large backhoe to skillfully correct problems. His father also knew how to do many onsite machine repairs and trained his mechanics daily. These skills and know-how allow the business owner to earn the respect and admiration of his employees, which is invaluable.

When thinking about buying or starting a business, a good idea is an honest assessment of your personal skills and interests. Most entrepreneurs naturally progress from an occupation as an employee into starting their own business in the same field. However, many owners merely buy a business or franchise that they deem lucrative. As mentioned in a previous chapter, basic accounting and financial skills are a must for any owner. Furthermore, the entrepreneur must get trained or licensed (if applicable) in their particular industry. Taking classes, obtaining certifications, and reading industry publications are imperative for a business owner to really understand, predict, and adapt to the constantly changing landscape inherent in all industries.

In choosing a business to start or purchase, I strongly suggest an industry in which you have a particular interest and skill. Additionally, your age and personal fitness should be considered in your assessment. If you have medical conditions or may be at an age where a business has physical requirements that you cannot endure, this needs to affect your decision process. Think about your personal skills and how they might affect your success. *Do you know how to use tools? Do you have a basic understanding of building and construction? Do you have medical training? How are your computer skills? Do you have any experience in the food industry?* These self-assessments should be conducted before embarking on a new business journey to avoid future pitfalls. I have a friend who took over as chief executive officer (CEO) of his family's car dealerships founded by his grandfather. I recall him once saying to me that he knows nothing about cars except how to drive them and count the money. That comment always stuck with me and popped into my head as

I met owners of businesses who know nothing about their product or service. They are truly doing a disservice to their employees, customers, and the business as a whole.

When to hire experts versus taking on business tasks yourself is another important personal skill assessment an entrepreneur must think about. When starting a business, money can be tight, and new owners tend to try and do everything themselves. When I was younger, I would move furniture, paint, run cabling, and do electric work, along with some construction during the setup of an office. As I am older now and suffer from lower back pain from degenerative discs, I have found the dollar cost of hiring professionals for these tasks is lower than the rehab and pain costs associated with my back problems. "Penny wise, pound foolish" is an old saying I think about often now regarding decisions. I recall a story that a friend managing a residential homebuilder business once told me. His job site supervisor on a neighborhood construction project would always focus on small tasks and miss the big picture. Once the supervisor spent his morning personally repairing a new homeowner's sink leak while several tons of gravel were being dumped in the wrong lot on the job site. The workers spent the next two days moving all of the rock to the correct location, which was quite costly in terms of labor and time. The small cost of a plumber to repair the sink was a better use of his time, as the job super should have been focusing on large and expensive construction supervision.

Other tasks requiring highly technical skills should be paid for by the new entrepreneur. Legal contract reviews, partnership agreements, and lease documents should be created or reviewed by trained lawyers. The Internet has numerous legal forms for download, but saving money up front on these important documents will inevitably cost time and money in the future when disputes arise. I recall writing my own partnership operating agreement modeled after one that I had downloaded. I asked a lawyer friend to review the document, and after a quick read, he told me there were big problems and it needed a lot of revision. I had him do the work, and luckily it only cost me a nice dinner and drinks. In retrospect, it was an excellent idea to have a trained lawyer review and rewrite this important document. Tax preparation and filings should also be done, in most cases, by a professional. It is easy to download online tax software and attempt to produce your own business tax returns. Still, I found the possibility of an audit and the time and costs associated with an improper tax filing are not worth the risk.

    Another task that professionals should be hired to complete is network and server setup. Most businesses are very reliant on their computer networks, and the risk of hackers and ransomware attacks has become more prevalent in today's world. A properly managed firewall and backed-up network will save a business owner immeasurable amounts of money and suffering. Think about what you can and cannot do in the setup of a business, and make sure your business plan has the correct budget for hiring experts.

Chapter 6 - Assets

Money is probably your best asset in starting a business, but entrepreneurs should think about other assets they possess or have access to when starting a new venture. The first important asset is a place to work. Most new ventures are initiated in the home. Whether it be just for the planning stages or the long-term goal of working and running a business from your home, the owner needs to think about the pros and cons of working where they live. I find working from home to be full of distractions but a bit better than a long commute to an office. An entrepreneur working in a small apartment with a spouse and possibly children along with several business partners might be untenable. In the fledgling stages of a business, the cost-saving and low-risk factors of launching from your home are attractive. A friend of mine started a woodworking business in his basement. As the business morphed from a hobby to a full-time money-making occupation, the constant loud noises from the saws and sanders became a nuisance to his family. Instead of renting a commercial workshop, he decided to build a detached garage woodshop in his backyard, allowing him to work at home without disturbing his family.

Access to commercial space to work is a big plus, especially if you can use the space without committing to a long-term commercial lease with high costs and guarantees. Borrowing a spare office from your rich uncle is a great low-risk strategy, but not always an option, which leads to paying rent for your start-up. Many commercial leases require the lessee to pay for enhancements and compliance with local building codes, along with the Americans with Disabilities Act. A friend of mine started a restaurant/catering service several years back and needed to pay for installing a commercial stove and refrigerator/freezer, and also was required to build two handicap-accessible bathrooms with wider doorways and ramp access. These upfront costs were quite large and saddled the business with too much debt from the start. It is always smarter to start small, borrow space from friends, and/or start working out of your house until you can prove your business concept and generate revenues.

When starting a new business, an owner's access to inexpensive assets can be very beneficial. Think about the needs of the business and what vehicles, tools, computer equipment, retail shelving, appliances, etc. you can use to start. A friend of mine lost his job in the wholesale fish industry and started a high-end seafood preparation and home delivery service. Instead of signing a lease with a commercial kitchen where he could prepare the fish, he negotiated with a local catering company to make use of their kitchen during idle hours and store items in their refrigerators. He could also obtain a certificate from the Department of Health with an established kitchen more easily. This agreement turned out to be mutually beneficial to both parties, and helped my friend start his business in a conservative and low-risk manner. A new business does not need to buy new equipment. Used appliances, tools, delivery vans, etc. are sold every day at wholesale auctions, on Craigslist, and are included many times with commercial leases. Do your research, call in favors, and borrow assets to launch your business in a conservative and cost-efficient manner to give it the best chance of success.

Chapter 7 - Business Type

All businesses are either service-oriented, product-based, or a hybrid in both categories. For example, a hair salon is generally considered a service-based enterprise because customers pay a stylist for their expertise and time. However, many salons encourage customers to buy hair products from their retail boutiques, making them a hybrid business. When assessing a venture, it is important for the entrepreneur to first think about service versus product and the inherent characteristics that come with each.

A service-based enterprise will require a laser focus on labor, as your business is solely reliant on the skills, expertise, and cost of your employees. The owner needs to hire and retain quality employees and pay them well, yet leave room for profit in the company's operation. A product-based business relies on supply chain, manufacturing, storage costs, and shipment to end consumers. An owner of a successful product-based business must be focused on manufacturing, supply sourcing, inventory levels, and shipping logistics. Both service and product-based ventures always rely on marketing and referrals, but more importantly, they must focus on sales. Other types of classifications covered in this chapter relate to industry-specific characteristics and the income business type.

Service-Based Businesses

Whenever I hear about service-based businesses, my initial thought is about management skills. An entrepreneur embarking on a service-based business needs to have superior people skills and the patience to deal with the problems that come with managing. A manager must walk a fine line between being efficient and business-focused while earning the respect and loyalty of his subordinates. This delicate balance is imperative in a service-based business for motivating your staff to work hard and help you build a successful and highly regarded five-star business. When employees are disgruntled and unhappy in their work, especially in a customer-facing, service-based business, the future is not promising. With the explosion of online reviews and customer ratings, an entrepreneur needs to make sure the staff providing their services is happy and portray a positive company image.

I recall having a problem with my home Internet and television service. After sitting on hold for an hour and finally getting a capable technology support person, there was a high level of frustration expressed by both the support person and me in dealing with the system architecture. The support person apologized, yet complained about how archaic the interface on her end operated and how long she would have to wait to get a hold of an engineer to fix the problem. She later arranged for a field technician to come to my home for a repair. The tech arrived late and began with an apology, and then he started complaining as well.

He told me that the company assigned too many jobs to him per day, and he could not possibly travel and make the repairs in the time allotted. He also said he was tired of dealing with angry and frustrated customers. As a business owner, the goal is to have an efficient business with happy and loyal employees. They need to be fulfilled in their daily jobs and portray a positive corporate image.

In general, service-based businesses can be split into professional and blue-collar classifications. A medical practice, a law or accounting firm, and an engineering design firm all tend to hire college-educated professionals requiring high-level certifications and licenses to perform their service. These professional, white-collar businesses tend to have much higher labor costs and generally require comprehensive medical benefits, 401k retirement plans, and annual salary/bonus structures for compensation and talent retention. These employees tend to be more static and retention is easier for the owner. A blue-collar, service-based business such as a home improvement company, auto service, or car wash tends to have lower labor costs, usually based on hourly wages, and includes few medical and other employment benefits. Even blue-collar-based businesses that require high-level certifications and training such as plumbers, welders, and electricians tend to earn hourly wages with little employment benefits, and therefore employees are quicker to leave for better opportunities. As an owner/manager, these inherent differences in types of service-based business need to be assessed and matched with your background and personal skill set.

Product-Based Businesses

Product-based businesses require personnel and payroll, but the focus is obviously on the merchandise, which requires special attention on inventory and related costs. A business owner in a product-based business has to manage supply costs to become profitable. These include transportation logistics on both obtaining supply from manufacturers and shipping to customers, as well as maintaining inventory and paying for storage. Inherent in supply management are the decay, obsolescence, damage, and costs of keeping enough product supply on hand to avoid delays in shipping or manufacturing. This is a tricky balance that requires an owner to be very detail-oriented. Whether the business is manufacturing and selling a product, or merely a reseller of a product online or in a retail storefront, the profit margins generally become compressed as the owner needs to move aged inventory.

Think about the type of inventory you are selling and the risks of decay, obsolescence, and cost of carry. A designer clothing store or shoe store always worries about this year's styles and moving last season's products. The risk of product decay versus shelf life should also be considered. A bakery or frozen yogurt store needs to throw out all unsold inventory, sometimes daily, versus a liquor store, for example. A liquor store can generally keep spirits and beer for sale for many months, even years.

There are many inherent risks in product-based businesses. Manufacturers tend to offer discounts at wholesale when resellers order larger quantities. These economies of scale allow major retailers like Walmart and Costco to sell at a lower retail price, giving them a large competitive advantage. However, these larger orders and discounts come with risks that must be weighed against potential gains. I recall a friend in the corporate premium logo business: a manufacturer and reseller of corporate mugs, pens, golf shirts, and other specific company logo items. Before the 2008 financial crisis, his largest client was Lehman Brothers, a large Wall Street brokerage firm. My friend would inventory large quantities of Lehman-engraved executive desk sets, mugs, golf balls, and gym bags along with other corporate products that would be given to Lehman employees as awards and to customers as gifts. These products were expensive to produce and store, but Lehman was a great client for these corporate premium items. This was a highly profitable business until Lehman went bankrupt, leaving my friend with unpaid invoices and expensive Lehman-specific inventory that was now worthless. It was a tough lesson to learn, but my friend recovered and his business is doing well.

  Some product-based businesses have a business model where they effectively never take possession of the product. Many products are now sold in this manner, where the customer orders an item from an intermediary, and the box is shipped directly from the manufacturer. This style of product-based business is very attractive as it takes out the risks and costs of inventory storage. I have a friend who works on websites and built a platform for a window shade and blinds company. The Web interface allows customers and home interior designers to shop styles and input window measurements. The website can take payment, and the orders are directly routed to the manufacturer for production. The blinds are then drop-shipped to the end user with the website business never taking possession of the merchandise, yet taking a substantial cut of the order revenue for making the sale. They only need to maintain a customer support call line for errors and returns, requiring minimal staff. This example always struck me as a really efficient and low-risk product-based business.

Lastly, when assessing a product-based business, think about the retail price, shipping, and returns. In an online-based business, shipping large and heavy products is onerous and costly for both the vendor and the end user. Expensive products are also more expensive to ship in terms of insurance and loss/theft, and tend to have higher customer return rates. Think about a product that costs the customer $200 versus $20. Any post-purchase cognitive dissonance *(a marketing term for a customer not totally happy with their purchase)* for the $200 item will surely lead to a return. A $20 item is far less likely to be returned, as the effort to package up and ship is not worth the time or money for the unhappy customer. Less expensive products with high profit margins shipped from an online store are attractive.

Hybrid Businesses

Many businesses tend to have a combination of both products and services to generate revenue. Some labor-oriented businesses have a product piece, where the customer is buying a product from the service provider such as a home contractor. In many cases, the contractor is paid for his expertise and time but is also purchasing building supplies at wholesale and up-charging the customer for these materials. An example of a true hybrid business is the restaurant industry. Customers pay for table service from the waiter and the chef's meal preparation and also pay the cost of the food purchased by the owner. As an industry, the costs in general at a restaurant are roughly split 50/50 between the price of labor and the cost of food. This type of hybrid business has many moving parts for the restaurant owner, including personnel management and retention, food supply and storage logistics, and a true reliance on customer reviews.

I have a friend who recently purchased a bar/restaurant that already had a presence and loyal customer base. The location of the operation and the track record of the revenues and profits made this a much-less risky endeavor versus constructing and starting a new restaurant from scratch. However, at almost 50 years old, my friend found himself working in the restaurant for very long shifts and managing personnel disputes and dealing with daily customer complaints. Refining the menu, managing food waste, and ordering all types of meats and produce, along with liquor and beer, is a full-time job. My friend is successful in his restaurant hybrid product and service business but often expresses his surprise at the complexity of a seemingly simple bar/restaurant.

Complex vs. Simple Businesses

Whether a product- or service-based business, the level of complexity is a facet a new owner should consider. As stated previously, operating a restaurant/bar is a very complex business, whereas selling a single product online is probably the simplest. There are many variations of complexity in terms of materials, labor, and reliance on others to complete a sale. For example, a bathroom remodeling contracting business has to deal with the homeowner's tastes and the wait for town permits, and sometimes relies on a previous contractor's work during the process. I recall renovating a bathroom, and the granite counter fabricator blamed the sheetrock installer for a curved wall. Then the shower glass contractor blamed the tile installer for uneven surfaces. Simple businesses where the owner controls the whole process from start to completion are always preferable.

Think about the business and all of the moving parts that are required. Operating a manufacturing business that makes too many SKUs

(Stock Keeping Units), maybe different colors, sizes, and quantities per package is sometimes overwhelming for a business. Selling or manufacturing a product that comes in one size and is for all genders is so much more simple. For example, compare a manufacturer of electric scooters versus a shoe company. Scooters are ubiquitous whereas shoes need to be made in multiple sizes, colors, and for each gender. Equivalently, a service provider who offers too many services may be too onerous and inefficient for the owner, as well. Think about the business in regard to middlemen, regulations, and multiple moving parts. My brother got involved in a trucking business and found this business to be quite complex. At first, he thought it was leasing the trucks, buying the trailers, hiring drivers, using a broker to dispatch loads, and getting paid. As it turns out, there were multiple pitfalls to the trucking business. Complex state rules and fines, and various types of loads requiring different straps and tarps were the norm. Daily traffic delays, truck-loading wait times, mechanical problems, and driver personal issues caused nonstop disruptions, requiring constant problem-solving by the owner. All of these issues reduced profitability and took just too much time, leading to the eventual closure of my brother's trucking business.

Industry

When looking at a new business, the entrepreneur should spend some time thinking about the industry and whether it is growing, stable, or declining. For example, a coin-operated laundry is a business that has been around for decades and is stable and consistent. Opportunity for high growth and innovation is minimal. In contrast, many businesses in the technology industry experience explosive growth. However, these high-growth businesses are saddled with intense competition for employees and customers along with an inherent risk to profitability and long-term survival. Some businesses operate in industries that are on the decline and should be avoided.

I recall working with a business broker in 1998 to look for a business to purchase. I met with an elderly man who ran a machine shop that made replacement parts for the large machines that make the glass tubes for florescent light bulbs. The owner had no children to take over this profitable business, and had a large client base and loyal employees working on the manufacturing floor. My initial thought was that this was a proven business in a great industry with few competitors. Upon further research and investigation into the light bulb industry of the late '90s, I found that a new technology in light bulbs was coming that produced more light with less heat, hence using less electricity. The new bulbs were called LED and would replace the old technology completely over time. These new LED bulbs did not require the glass from the florescent glass-making machinery, which was probably the true reason this business was for sale. Luckily, I did my research.

Margin & Turnover

An important aspect of business that is often overlooked is to assess profit margin and turnover for both a service- and a product-based company. For example, a luxury jewelry store sells high-margin items, normally at double their cost or a 50 percent profit margin. However, it takes quite a long time to sell one high-end item, leading to a long turnover time. During this time, the jeweler must either finance or pay for the opportunity cost of holding onto that expensive item while trying to sell it. In comparison, a hardware store that sells nuts and bolts might sell lots of inventory each day, leading to high turnover at a low-profit margin. Inherent to specific industries is a general level of margin and turnover, but you need to assess this important aspect as a prospective business owner.

Within industries, different styles of similar businesses have varying degrees of margin and turnover. For example, a residential driveway paving company operates on a high margin, yet a low turnover. Most homeowners repave their driveway only once every 15 years. However, a driveway sealing company will seal the blacktop every other year, leading to a higher turnover but a lower profit margin. An ideal business has a service or a product with a higher profit margin and high turnover rates. Think about a business with customers who often come for your service or product and one that you earn a healthy profit margin on each sale.

Rental Businesses

The rental industry is a business type that bridges both product and service. A business in the rental industry provides the owner with recurring income, which is appealing, yet comes with upfront investment and ongoing management. The basic categories of rental income come from either residential or commercial investments, but there are many sub-categories in each and other businesses that are effectively rental businesses.

In the residential space, the owner buys a property and rents it to people to live in. It seems obvious and simple, but there are many aspects to think about in this type of business. First, the owner must decide on financing, to either purchase the property outright or, the more common method, take a bank mortgage. After the owner does a financial analysis, the overriding theme is to have tenants pay monthly rent that pays off the mortgage. Over time, the property is paid off, hopefully appreciated, and the owner has a fully paid asset that still generates monthly income. It sounds great, but there are risks and headaches. My brother got into the Section-8 rental business, which involves buying homes in lower-income areas where renters are given government support from the Department of Housing & Urban Development (HUD). The appeal of this type of residential rental business is that the government pays the rent, thereby reducing the risk of collection. However, my brother spends inordinate amounts of time on rental turnovers, which is common in this low-income type of rental. Tenants are more transient, and the space needs to be shown often and cleaned/painted for new tenants.

Additionally, there are generally missed months of rent during the transition of tenants. My brother-in-law owns some residential rental homes, as well, and I recall one problem he encountered. He had to spend months in court evicting a nonpaying tenant, which was time-consuming and costly. Most municipalities are very tenant-friendly and are reluctant to throw families to the street. When he was finally victorious in court and able to evict the tenant, to his dismay, he found the angry tenant moved out and left a running garden hose in the basement window. Unable to prove that the disgruntled tenant caused the damage, my brother-in-law had to replace the home furnace and air conditioning unit and have the basement dried out. Most residential real estate investors enjoy speaking about their terrific investments but tend not to bring up the unrented months, eviction legal costs, high maintenance effort, and time spent.

Operating a rental business in the commercial space alleviates some of the issues of residential rentals, such as evicting families, lower renter turnover as leases tend to be longer term, and the constant maintenance headaches. Generally, commercial tenants are responsible for equipment and property maintenance and tend to invest in the property to make it work for their specific business. The recurring income model of the commercial rental is attractive, yet there are more months of vacancies during the transition of renters. My friend owns and rents commercial stores in a high-traffic area. The business is generally profitable and the rent is usually easily collected. Issues related to roof leaks and building air conditioning units have been the only small issues until the recent COVID-19 pandemic. Many commercial tenants stopped paying rent, which most real estate investors faced. This just emphasizes how this type of business is subject to economic recession and depression risks. These are highly infrequent events that must be assessed and weighed against the amount of cash, leverage, and liquidity that the commercial business owner can access.

There are many other rental-style businesses, such as cars, bikes, tools, and equipment. All have the same general characteristics of upfront costs, maintenance, and loss of income during nonrental periods. I have a friend who got involved in the Uber car rental business. With the explosive growth in Uber, my friend realized that potential Uber drivers could not afford the upfront payment or lacked proper credit to sign a car lease. He purchased ten black Toyota Camrys and set up a monthly rental business for drivers. After advertising and locking in leases with drivers, his Uber rental business was producing income. He did incur some maintenance headaches, the occasional driver using the car for personal long trips, and some downtime with storage problems of the unused cars. The business was profitable until the recent COVID-19 pandemic. He, along with investors in Airbnb rental homes, all saw their profitable rental business rapidly decline due to forces beyond their control. Once again, conservative growth and maintaining cash liquidity to get through unexpected turbulence are imperative in these rental-type businesses. Luckily, my friend benefited from the explosion in used car prices during the pandemic and was able to quickly sell his ten used cars with ease.

Chapter 8 - Location

Location, location, location is so often spoken about when opening a retail store. I like to think of the term "location" regarding a new business a bit differently. When assessing a business, think about the location *needs*. Do you want to be involved in a business that has a prestigious retail city location with super high rent or would you prefer a low-cost warehouse location outside of a city? I walk by many New York City 5th Avenue retail jewelry stores and always think about how much money the owner is paying each day for that location. I ponder the carrying costs of the expensive jewelry, the well-dressed staff salaries, and the electric bill, in addition to that enormous rent versus how many jewelry items they sold that day. It seems like a very tough business where your major cost is rent and you have a huge daily operating loss each morning when you turn on the lights. Think about your other overhead costs when thinking about location. Not only does a prestigious location cost more in rent, but it also requires more in overall operating costs. Staff salaries, utility bills, construction and maintenance costs, and food options for staff all tend to be much higher in the center of a city. Does your business need this location?

When you think about a location, do your research. You must find out what businesses were previously in that space and why they moved or failed. I am always perplexed when a retail furniture store fails, and then another ambitious owner opens *another* furniture store in the same location. And then it fails. Research a retail location before signing a lease. Find out how staff will commute to the location, where they will park and eat lunch. These factors greatly affect the quality of the staff and the future of the business. Do surveillance on the foot traffic on various days of the week if you are looking at opening a retail store. Is there an anchor store (i.e. a well-known franchise) that draws customers to the location? Is the town friendly toward businesses in terms of its ordinances and building codes? Also, what competition to your business is nearby? A competent commercial real estate broker should be able to answer many of these questions, but you must conduct your own due diligence, as well.

It always makes sense to speak with other tenants in a prospective location to assess the landlord and building infrastructure. I recall speaking with one tenant in a building in New York City who informed me that the building had terrible electrical problems and constant Internet outages. The broker neglected to do this research for me. This was quite useful information to eliminate that location for my computer-based trading company. At another building, a neighboring tenant to the space I was viewing told me the Korean restaurant below made use of heavy amounts of garlic starting at about 10am every morning, which was unbearable. That piece of information ruled out that location. And lastly, I spoke with one tenant in a building who told me the air conditioning system was terrible and the landlord was unresponsive to requests to remedy the problem. Research and speaking with people are so important in assessing a location for your business to prevent future headaches.

Chapter 9 - Customers

Customers are the key to the success of your business. The type of customer and how you interact with them should be assessed in detail. The first major classification is whether they are a commercial or a retail/residential customer. A friend of mine who runs a landscaping company started his business mowing lawns, which was the gateway to getting residential paver patio and landscaping jobs. However, he found that dealing with homeowners was too cumbersome in terms of design decisions, constant complaints, and changes during construction, along with troubles collecting payment. He eventually decided to focus only on commercial business. This shift allowed for a larger revenue and profit per job and fewer headaches. As you assess your business, think about who your main customer will be, and if you have the interpersonal skills and patience to deal with a retail customer base.

Interactions with customers can be a large or small part of your business. Compare a retail store versus an online website, or a commercial versus residential contracting business. When you deal with individual homeowners and retail customers, you must be prepared to engage in cordial conversations and be patient while listening to the occasional verbose client. Rushed contractors and curt retail salespeople tend to earn negative reviews and therefore hurt future business referrals. Think about how your business will deal with customers and take an honest assessment of your interpersonal skill set. Of course, a retail chain of stores could have an owner who never speaks to a customer, but most new ventures need to start with the owner being the face of the business.

All classifications of customers should be considered as you think about your business. If you interact with customers, are you better suited to deal with professional white-collar clientele or blue-collar types? Are you good at dealing with older clients or would you prefer a business focused on children? As previously mentioned, do you want to deal with customers when they are happy and celebrating or are you a compassionate person able to be supportive of customers planning a funeral for a loved one or enduring pain related to sickness or rehab? Maybe you do not want to interact personally with customers at all, and then an online or phone-oriented business is more suitable.

I have always been averse to side businesses that focus on selling to family and friends as the primary customer base. It is one thing to ask family and friends for support and patronage when launching a new business, versus relying on them as the sole customer base. I recall being on the sidelines at my child's soccer game, and another father began soliciting parents on the bleachers to try his "revolutionary" new vitamin gummies. Not only was he trying to sell his product, but he was also recruiting other parents to become salespeople in his multi-level marketing business (MLM). Many people find these MLM businesses a good way to supplement their primary income, and some have grown their network into large, successful, primary incomes. In my life, I have been approached by family and friends selling everything from Amway products, various skin creams/vitamins, high-end gym apparel, and even sex toys. Most of these MLM businesses encourage recruiting and selling to family and friends to build your business to achieve a residual income. The pyramid structure of the MLM business tends to be most lucrative for the person at the top of the structure. Think about your business and how you want people to perceive you when assessing what type of customer base you need to build a successful endeavor.

Chapter 10 - Partners/Employees

Who you work with on a daily basis is a serious consideration when starting a business. The initial decision is to assess if you need a partner and what type of employees you would like to have work for you. There are many factors to consider, and with both partners and employees, your personal characteristics and the type of business you are starting will strongly dictate your decisions.

In terms of partners, most young entrepreneurs develop a business idea with a friend, coworker, or spouse, and move forward without really thinking about who they are getting into business with. Unfortunately, the majority of partnerships end badly as the business matures. If the business is successful, one of the partners undoubtedly will think their contributions and efforts are invaluable, which leads to conflict. If the business is struggling or fails, the finger-pointing between the partners always results in a fight, especially when money, family, or spouses are involved. I cannot stress enough to assess a partner and the real business need to have that partner. Can the business start without one of you? Does your prospective partner have skills, talents, or industry licenses that are critical to the business? Who is bringing the seed investment capital to the business and is the equity ownership commensurate with the risk of losing that capital? Do you want to be in business with your relative, best friend, or significant other? Do you work well together? Ask yourself these questions and <u>really</u> spend time thinking about the answers.

    My father-in-law started a life insurance brokerage business with a partner early on in his career. The two partners shared the office rent, the salary of their secretary, and other office expenses, and covered for one another when either was out on a client visit or on vacation. The partnership worked well for years until the business became successful and the partners began arguing about who was bringing in more revenue. One partner had previously created more of the revenue, but now the tables had turned. Further, my father-in-law's partner began using the company expense account for personal flights and lunches, which led to more conflict. After a legal battle, they eventually split the partnership and parted ways with very hard feelings. A costly and stressful separation that hurt the business could have been avoided. In retrospect, they should have had a clear operating agreement to clarify each partner's responsibilities, how to allocate revenue and expenses, and a specific process for termination of the partnership. I have seen many partnerships, such as sports management agencies, law firms, dental practices, accounting firms, and bars/restaurants that have all fallen prey to fights between the owners. The common theme for this conflict stems from each partner thinking they are working harder and are more valuable and deserving of a larger share of the profits. Some thought, legal planning, and finding a partner with a similar work ethic and the same goals for the business are imperative from the start.

In terms of employees, think about who you would like to work and spend your time with. Are you interested in working with college-educated professionals such as those at a wealth management or accounting firm? Or do you like working with a lower-educated and blue-collar workforce as you might find at a car wash or a construction business? Do you want your business to rely on teenage employees such as those at fast-food and retail chains? There are reliable, ethical, and hard-working employees in both white- and blue-collar businesses, but I have found there tends to be more employee turnover in the latter. Assess if you can manage and communicate with these various types of employees. I recall a friend who owned a local salad shop in addition to her full-time job as a nurse. In the hospital nursing profession, she would have several long shifts followed by a couple of days off per week. The salad shop was a side business she could manage during those free days and earn extra income with hopefully little stress. However, that was not the case. Many days, the manager and/or several of the teenage workers would call in sick, and the salad chopping and preparation would need to be done by an overqualified hospital nurse, aka the owner. She eventually sold the business. This type of daily stress and employee unreliability are inherent in so many businesses and need to be factors in your assessment of business fit.

In terms of employee reliability and loyalty, a factor that also requires thought is employee turnover, which occurs in all types of businesses. I recall hiring a college graduate as a trading assistant and thinking he was a liability as I trained him. It took quite a while until he became a useful asset who I could rely on to help with my daily duties. However, when my assistant left for a better opportunity after I spent countless hours training and teaching, I recall being furious and feeling betrayed. I was always reluctant to impart my time and knowledge to future assistants for fear of them leaving and wasting my efforts. However, as a business owner, this balance of training and time investment in employees versus the turnover rate requires analysis. Employees generally focus on doing what is best for them versus what is best for your business. As an owner, you must remember that fact.

Some industries make use of union employees. When assessing a new venture, be aware of the risk of union labor with regard to long-term contracts, loss of negotiating power, and the control of your workforce. During the recent COVID-19 pandemic, employees were hard to acquire and therefore made more demands on their employers. During this labor scarcity, unions were able to make quite high demands that remained in effect long after the labor supply constraints subsided.

Another topic requiring thought when hiring staff is whether they will be full-time employees, part-time workers, contractors, or interns. As an owner, you need to look at your business needs, state regulations regarding employees, and what types of benefits you will offer. Many businesses pay their employees "off-the-books," which is not legal. I recommend playing by the rules and paying employees according to state laws. Paying legitimate, documented employees with a W-2 and workers comp insurance via an official payroll relieves your company of risks down the road. Plan to be successful and conduct your venture with integrity. Assessing if you can employ part-time staff with no benefits versus paying them as contractors or consultants is a matter specific to your particular business and state regulation. It is best to be conservative in your hiring when starting an endeavor, as it is always easier to hire more staff than to let people go if the fledgling business hits any financial speed bumps.

Consider hiring college interns who generally work for free, yet can be valuable in helping you build your company. The relationship between a business and a "free" intern is generally mutually beneficial as the business obtains free labor. The intern obtains experience and this helps build their resume for future employment. Also, make use of freelance website services such as Upwork and Fiverr. These websites match talent with specific jobs at either hourly or project based rate structures. I personally made use of these types of services to edit this book and found the work to be excellent and the costs extremely fair.

Lastly, when embarking on a technology-based or innovative new venture, many highly valued, day-one employees working for free tend to hope for large equity stakes in the future. I have seen staff donating their time and sweat equity to an app, website, or new technology they deeply believe in with the hopes of a venture capital firm coming in and funding the enterprise. As the owner/founder, I strongly encourage you to spend a bit of time communicating with your staff what your expectations are and what they should expect. Too many successful enterprises fail due to key personnel who expect huge equity stakes and big payouts, and leave when they are disappointed. Communication is key from the start.

Chapter 11 - Marketing

Getting the word out about your new business is difficult and expensive. Many people spend time and money coming up with an innovative product or new service but neglect a well-thought-out marketing plan. A retail storefront in a highly visible location effectively has a marketing expense built into the rent, but a service-based business or online store needs to be publicized. Buying a franchise or a business that already has a loyal customer base is the simplest in terms of marketing. It allows the new owner to focus on the business without immediately spending on advertising.

    The first step in marketing your new business is the name and logo. Since this is the branding and image of your business, it needs to be simple to quickly convey what your business does. I have seen so many company names, store signage, and brandings that tell nothing about the business and leave me confused. Your potential customers are all busy with their lives; they need a clear and quick understanding of what your logo and catchphrase are selling with no ambiguity. However, trying to find a short four or five-letter name like Uber is extremely difficult to create a brand around. Currently the word "Uber" is a universal colloquialism to mean a private personal taxi, but initially the company was called Ubercab, meaning a cab "above the rest." Only when the term became a common name for a private cab did the company shorten its official name. A new business owner cannot attempt to emulate the naming success of Uber. Keep the name and logo simple, yet descriptive enough so that customers have a clue what your business is selling.

    Every business owner needs to market and sell. Even a dentist, a tax accountant, and an air conditioning repair service must market and then make a sale. There is a difference between brand image and awareness, advertising, and actually creating sales revenue. People with introverted personalities who decide to open their own businesses need to realize they will be selling. You can hire people to help, but as the owner, you will be the new business marketing team and sales force leader, as it is your capital and your success at stake. Starting off marketing to friends and family and asking them for help in spreading the word is the normal, easy path for most new start-ups, but that avenue fizzles quickly. My favorite method of marketing is referrals and positive buzz. If the product or service is truly great and provides value to customers, the marketing costs should be minimal and the sales should come more easily.

    Giving away free samples, conducting free seminars, and attempting to get free publicity is a good start to marketing your new business. We all like "free", but remember that your time and free samples do cost money. The publicity route is an effective marketing tool. Be sure to create a well-written and concise press release for emailing to local newspapers and television broadcasts. Many local news outlets are always looking for short human-interest stories in their town but are pretty sharp in filtering out those looking for free advertising. There needs to be a good story angle in your press release and a captivating email header when contacting news editors.

Coming up with a creative or quirky video or an ad campaign with the hopes of going viral and being seen on the Internet is always a long shot. I also find search engine optimization (SEO) where your website is slated to come up on the first page of a search engine to be important, but this is explained and covered in many other resources, so I will not cover it here. I will say that the companies that advertise this SEO service are quite expensive, so do your research and spend conservatively. The targeted niche ads offered on Facebook, Instagram, Google, and other social media tend to also be expensive but do allow the business owner to serve their message to a specifically filtered audience. These ads may obtain clicks to your website or app but don't necessarily convert into customers and sales.

Craft-oriented websites such as Etsy and Pinterest are useful for some businesses but are not necessarily the platform for a growing professional business. My friend who markets his woodworking business uses a website called Custom Made from which he obtains multiple inquiries from his photo gallery and reviews of his past work. Ebay, Ioffer, and other selling style websites also are good venues to market and sell your products but are very product-specific and generally do not help a business owner build their brand.

I always avoid trying the easy and cheap method of sending spam emails or participating in robocalling. These inferior marketing tactics just prove to be annoying to the public and tarnish your new business's reputation. Do small tests and find marketing tactics that work. For example, sponsor a local sports team or school program, or try the local Penny Saver or Val-Pak mailers. My friend who owns a patio paver sealing company once told me he does quite well in our town with these mailers. But you need to be cognizant of your business matching your advertising medium. Do customers look in the Penny Saver or direct mailers for a lawyer or a high-end niche product? Probably not. Those businesses might be better served with advertisements in various newspapers or industry-specific publications or magazines. In terms of marketing a specific product or service, consider renting a booth at an industry-related expo. Spend conservatively and test various marketing options until you find the most value for your marketing dollar.

Online reviews have become the most effective tool for prospective customers to evaluate your product or service. We have all seen websites such as Google, Amazon, Walmart, and Yelp that have one- to five-star ratings with written reviews from customers. The reviews that sometimes include photos greatly influence new customers. As a new business, doing your best to provide a good product or service with ample customer support is imperative to having a positive customer experience. Your product or service will be reviewed, and these criticisms or compliments are quite important to future sales. These reviews are permanent on the Internet for all to see. Even though many customers are picky, annoying, and unfair in their requests, the customer is always right. As a new business owner, you must remember to do your best to keep your customers happy—as they are your best marketing assets.

Chapter 12 - Risks

I wrote most of this book during my free time at home during the COVID-19 pandemic of 2020–23. This unseen risk has proven to be fatal to many longstanding successful businesses. Most businesses related to the travel and leisure industries, including restaurants, movie theaters, hotels, airlines, and cruises were battered, with revenues falling off a cliff. The employees in these industries and ancillary businesses were also greatly harmed in this unrelenting and depressing pandemic. For example, a retail store in a previously high-traffic airport and a successful t-shirt shop near a concert/sports arena both shuttered their business, furloughed their employees, and could not pay their rent or mortgages. As a business owner, planning for the risk of a pandemic was impossible. However, maintaining liquidity and creativity in your ability to pivot your business when faced with adversity allows the best businesses to prevail when the downturn subsides.

In every industry, there are winners and losers when catastrophe strikes. For example, during the COVID-19 pandemic, bars and sit-down dining suffered immensely while package liquor stores, grocery chains, and take-out dining venues did well. Some restaurants tried to pivot and convert from inside tables to tent dining and take-out orders but still only earned a fraction of their previous revenues. My brother-in-law owns a contract cleaning business that provides mid-sized office cleaning services. During the pandemic, these offices were all closed and workers were mandated to work from home, rendering his office cleaning services unnecessary. However, another division of his business cleans the entry lobbies and elevators of local apartment buildings. He was luckily able to increase sanitizing and cleaning services at these buildings to make up for some lost office cleaning revenues. As a business owner, you must be flexible and stay in tune with what is going on in your industry and the risks in the overall economy. Always think about all the standard life clichés such as "Save for a rainy day" and "Hope for the best, but prepare for the worst."

Profit Margin Risk

Profit margin risk is just as important as risk to gross sales. Margin compression can come from either the sales side, the cost side, or possibly both. Sales pricing pressure emanates from the overall economy, industry, and competitive forces. Cost increases can arise from shortages, raw material price increases, and regulation changes. A business owner in both a service- or product-oriented business must assess this duality of risks. For example, my friend owns a bar/restaurant that is known for the best hamburger in Staten Island, NY. During the COVID-19 pandemic, he needed to pivot his establishment to outdoor dining and take-out orders. His sales revenue suffered similar to most restaurants, but also his costs started rising as meat prices surged due to pandemic-related shortages as a result of meat-packing plant closures. Raising prices to the customers was always an option, but he feared alienating his loyal customers who were not even dining inside his establishment. This profit-margin compression is a risk that can be detrimental to a successful business and usually rears its head at the worst times.

Sticky Brand Loyal Customers

Customer loyalty is valuable to most businesses to get them through trying times, but "sticky customer" businesses are also preferable. A residential pesticide company has little "stickiness" in its customer base. There is no real loyalty and customers can easily change their monthly service when approached by a lower-priced competitor. There is no luxury brand name in the pest industry. However, think about the home alarm business. The installed keypads, motion sensors, phone system central station monitoring, and home automation are more ingrained and difficult for residential customers to make a switch to a competitor. Companies like ADT can rely on these monthly residual revenues with little risk of customers fleeing to a competitor.

Apple has mastered the customer "stickiness" concept. Anyone who owns and uses technology in the Apple ecosystem knows how difficult it is to switch to a competitor for technology so rooted in our everyday lives. In terms of product brands, consider the example of Canada Goose down jackets. These down jackets have been around for decades, yet Canada Goose created a prestigious brand around their logo as a symbol of quality and luxury. When looking at new businesses, think about loyalty, branding, and the risk of customers easily switching to a competitor.

Competition Risk

Competition, in general, is a risk to your business. Are there any barriers to entry for a potential competitor to your business? Whether a service business, retail or online, or manufacturing a product, think about how many current and future competitors you may have. When investing in a retail location, a new business owner must think about this risk. Many anchor businesses in strip mall shopping centers in America are keen on this risk and contract with commercial owners to prevent other stores in the same shopping center that sell direct-competing products. I recall looking into opening a coffee/gelato cafe in a local strip mall with a Wawa food mart as the anchor store. The leasing agent told me he could not have any coffee, ice cream, or sandwich shops open in that strip mall as the Wawa lease contract strictly forbade competition. The larger franchises always seem to obtain these strategic advantages when contracting with their vendors and commercial leases, but you as a new business owner should think about this type of competition. How easily can a larger competitor open up nearby? Can your pricing be easily undercut by a larger competitor with economies of scale? What steps can you take to prevent competition?

There are many ways to protect your business from competition risks. In terms of a new product-based business, filing a utility or design patent is a logical protection, but these filings are generally quite expensive. My first utility patent cost $10,000 with legal and filing fees. As an inventor with a patent, you have to be willing to defend the patent if a product is successful and you have infringement claims against violators. This process is expensive in terms of legal fees and time. Filing a product trademark that is synonymous with your product also offers some level of protection. When you think of certain names and logos such as the Nike "swoosh" or the Coca-Cola logo, you instantly think of their brand and quality.

Another way to protect a new business from the risk of competition is with first-mover advantages. Being the first to market with your product or service is a key advantage that gives your business brand recognition and a head start against competitors in terms of know-how. Think about Amazon when it launched as a seller of online books. Barnes and Noble was clearly the largest and most well-known retail bookstore around, yet Amazon was able to get such a foothold in the online book space that no one could catch up. Amazon's technology and shipping logistics made them unbeatable, which they exploited to become the largest online seller of everything and anything. First-mover advantages are very important in minimizing competitive risks.

Regulation and Zoning Risks

Risks stemming from regulations, town zoning laws, inspections, and licensing are important to assess before embarking on a new business. Many new retail locations, especially those with traffic, parking, or drive-thru considerations must go through town planning and zoning committees. Recent new regulations about indoor dining, social distancing, face masks, and heating, ventilation, and air-conditioning (HVAC) filtration systems related to the recent COVID-19 pandemic will undoubtedly need to be considered long after this crisis has fully subsided. Some of these regulations and zoning rules are helpful to businesses in alleviating the risk of new competitors and some are not. For example, if you owned a liquor license or a taxi cab medallion, you were afforded a certain level of protection from competition. These items were deemed to be valuable assets to your business. Our town had a limited number of liquor licenses available to restaurants, just as New

York City had a limited number of taxi medallions. However, once a new administration came in and expanded liquor licenses or technological advances enabled companies like Uber to replace taxis, your valuable asset was suddenly vastly depreciated.

Another risk emanates from zoning/planning changes in a town. I recall a well-located Wendy's franchise that had a very busy drive-thru and therefore a successful business. After some years, the main highway in front of the Wendy's was rerouted with a bridge and jug-handle road turn-offs, making the restaurant difficult to access. A year later, the Wendy's was out of business. Many of these risks are unknown, unpredictable, and difficult to plan for but should be considered and analyzed. Some municipalities and states are easier than others for certain types of businesses. Do your research.

Recession and Liquidity Risks

As you assess various businesses to start or purchase, I recommend thinking about how the sales revenues are generated and if they are a luxury or a necessity for your customer base. In times of economic prosperity, customers spend on luxury items more freely, yet quickly tighten their belts when the economy turns down. Is your business prepared to handle these economic recession risks, and if you needed to sell your business in the future, how hard would it be?

Until this most recent recession in 2020 related to the COVID-19 pandemic, the economy had been growing since 2008. Those twelve years saw an economic expansion in most products and services. People readily spend $150 on dinners, $1,000 on smartphones for each of their family members (including their young children), and sometimes over $10,000 on family vacations. This spending shut off as the COVID-19 pandemic destroyed the economy. However, many necessities were still purchased. Home and auto maintenance, groceries, medical services, prescriptions, and insurance spending continued. As you assess a business, think about how your sales revenues are tied to the economy and the basic necessities of your customers.

Access to liquidity is important in your personal and business life. Unknown expenses can come from anywhere, and as a new business owner, you must have access to money. In terms of risk, a business owner should think about how hard it would be to sell the business if life circumstances required a liquidation. Also, assess how tied you as the owner are to the business. For example, a friend of mine sold his pain management business to a larger medical company. Part of the deal required him to work for several years during the transition to retain the customer base and earn his payout on the sale of the business. Another friend of mine was forced to sell his dental practice in a rushed manner due to personal reasons and had to take a considerable discount on the value of the business. When assessing businesses, think about the ease of exit if you need to sell in the future.

Other Risks to Consider

There are numerous other risks to consider in assessing a new business. A prospective owner needs to analyze their personal risk tolerance. Are you willing to risk a substantial amount of your personal assets in the purchase or the start-up of a new business? Using OPM (Other People's Money) is another option but usually comes with costs and strings attached. Also, it is a good idea to firewall your business from your personal assets and possibly your other businesses. I recall my father's friend owned several Burger King franchises. Each restaurant was structured as a separate Limited Liability Corporation (LLC). This setup not only protected each business from one another in terms of lawsuits (many retail businesses are sued for slips/falls, etc.), but allowed him to sell one restaurant at a time, which he did as he got older.

Another risk to consider is the weather. Is your business affected by severe weather (e.g. rain/flooding, power outages, wildfires, and hurricanes)? I have seen so many restaurants and stores get destroyed by flash floods in areas that never flooded. Friends of mine lost warehouses, vans, and all sorts of inventory and tools to water events. Mother Nature is tough to predict, but establishing your business on high ground away from rivers and the ocean, and away from high-risk fire zones is something to consider.

There are numerous other risks in starting a new business, but life, in general, has inherent risks. Over-analysis of risk might prevent many aspiring entrepreneurs from taking the leap, so be cognizant of the risks and do your best to minimize them. I always think about the owners of Blockbuster video rental franchises. The technology changed to allow streaming and on-demand movies, thereby making these rental businesses extinct. I also think about Tower Records, a huge New York-based record and music chain that has also gone the way of the dinosaur with the emergence of online music downloads. Technological advancements made these businesses obsolete; however, the owners had decades of success. In many cases, this type of success is a once-in-a-lifetime opportunity making the owners rich for life, so do not be over-cautious.

One last note on risk: Keep your personal beliefs and political opinions separate from your new business. It is too easy to alienate customers who disagree with your politics or opinions. Avoid flags, slogans, or any social media posts for your business related to politics, religion or high profile social issues. Remember the famous quote from Michael Jordan stating that "Republicans buy sneakers too". As an entrepreneur starting and building a successful business, there is no upside to the risk of offending any potential customer. Stay neutral and keep your focus on building your business.

Chapter 13 - Future

When you are assessing buying or starting a new business, the last thing you are thinking about is the future of a business that has not even been initiated. I am not suggesting spending a lot of time on this topic; however, there are some things to think about in terms of the future and longevity of your business. Is this a business that you can run as you get older and do you want to? Is this a business you would aspire for your children to take over one day, and do they have the skills to operate your business? Is your business scalable? You definitely need to focus on getting your new business operational and successful in the short run, but as you look at opportunities, think a bit about the future.

Family businesses sound great on the surface. We all have a sentimental thought when we hear from an owner that his great grandfather founded the business or we see a sign that says "family owned since 1925." These are great legacy business stories that owners can be proud of, yet we don't see a sign that says "Family business that incurred legal battles between the siblings and their spouses for years." A little sarcasm here, but you must realize that family businesses tend to be recipes for fights and hard feelings. Working with your siblings, spouse, parents, or children can be fun and endearing, but I have heard so many horror stories leading to families not speaking and expensive court battles. Think about if you want your family involved financially in your business. Really think about it.

As you look at a business, think about the future in terms of scalability. Some businesses are just not suited to be larger, either due to the owner being specifically needed for the business or there just not being enough demand. An encounter I recall that exemplifies both of these constraints is when I met an older man at a bar at the top of the Grand Canyon in Arizona. After a drink or two, the older gentlemen and I started chatting. He told me he was from Montana and worked as a wood "wheelwright". I had no idea what that meant and asked him to clarify. He had learned the very niche skill of straightening and repairing wooden wagon wheels. I tried to inquire—without sarcasm—if there was much demand for the repair of carriage wheels in this day and age. He replied that he was quite busy. People from all over the country would ship their wooden wheels to him for repair. As you are probably thinking right now as you read these words, my thought was, "Who still uses a horse-drawn carriage other than maybe the Amish people?" I concluded that this business was not scalable and really required the specific skill of the owner.

Expertise in running your business and economies of scale can be very favorable to future scalability. Only by experience will an owner learn the valuable details of how to run that specific business successfully. This experience will allow an entrepreneur to replicate and expand to other locations, regions, and possibly other countries. Look at the example of Starbucks. Founded in Seattle by a commercial coffee machine salesman, the branding, process, and defined menu made the business a huge success that expanded to numerous US cities and then worldwide. Scalability can also be achieved via acquisitions of competitors to achieve efficiencies from economies of scale. I have a friend who bought an existing lawn irrigation installation and maintenance company. Over time, he learned the business and achieved success. He then purchased several other small, local sprinkler companies for the valuable client base with its annual sprinkler opening/closing revenue stream. Using a single depot for equipment and vehicle storage, and a single office for billing and payroll clerical duties, he achieved more efficiency and profitability with far lower costs. A new business owner should always focus on the present to refine and build their new business, but keep an eye on the future.

Conclusion

After reading this book, one might ask...What is the perfect business? This question can only be answered by you. Further, as the owner grows in age and experience, the perfect business metric may change. In general, I feel that a financially successful business that affords the owner and their family a comfortable lifestyle is very important, yet not the sole criterion. Finding a business that you can build and enjoy working at every day should be your primary focus. Forging relationships with employees and customers while earning their loyalty and respect is worth more than money alone. Being a pillar in the community and building a legacy business that is not only financially successful but ethical should be your goal.

When I think of the ideal business, I think of low stress and fun. I do not mind hard work but want to avoid conflict, problems, and drama in my daily work life. Doing the right thing and providing a fair and valuable product or service to your customers is the first step. As mentioned in the book, I dealt with inferior products that I had manufactured in China. It was my fault for not having the products inspected before shipping across the ocean, but I refused to sell them to customers. Had I moved forward with the defective merchandise, I undoubtedly would have had complaints. Whether embarking on a product- or service-based business, do a good job, provide a quality product, and return customer calls and emails. I have dealt with so many business owners in my life who do not return calls and avoid customer queries and complaints. In this age of Internet reviews and social media, word travels fast, so run a good, honest business. Treat your customers and employees well, produce a valuable product, and as a business owner, stand by your work. Remember, a bad reputation and detrimental Internet reviews are permanent.

  Since I wrote the majority of this book during the COVID-19 pandemic, it made me think about risks to businesses. This unrelenting pandemic caused government-mandated shutdowns, and some businesses had to obtain Congressional funding via the Paycheck Protection Plan (PPP). Some businesses will survive with help, but many will shut their doors forever. The pandemic mostly damaged the travel and leisure industries. The employees were furloughed or permanently let go as these businesses failed with no revenue. Ancillary businesses and their employees also were severely affected. Think about those in the arena lighting business, cruise line food and transport, hotel towel companies, and retail stores and restaurants near these venues and reliant on tourism. They all suffered. There is no way to predict or fully prepare for this type of devastation, but many owners needed to make the tough decision to close their doors.

  This brought me to my next thought on risk and failure: knowing when to shut down your business. Pride and fear of embarrassment to your family and friends, along with loyalty to your employees, sometimes must be overcome by a business owner in a failing business. Doing your best to work hard and pivot your business when faced with insurmountable barriers to success is admirable, but knowing when to throw in the towel is vital. I always remember the cliché of "throwing good money after bad." As a business owner, investing more of your personal capital or risking your home or personal financial future must be avoided when a business has no chance of surviving. Many people look to the past success of their business and hope and pray for things to revert. Hoping and praying are not the traits of an owner with business acumen. As an owner of a failing business, you must decide when to close the doors. Use what you learned and preserve your personal capital and resources for your next business venture. Remember the old quote, "Failure is not a crime. Failure to learn from failure is." Learn, preserve capital, and move on.

    I have tried and failed at many business ventures per Chapter 2 of this book. My current business in the U.S. Treasury market has operated concurrently with most of these businesses since 2003, which has provided me with a constant income. This is a luxury that I have been fortunate to have, as many new entrepreneurs do not. Running a profitable proprietary trading business remains my most successful business venture. Besides my experience and skills in bond trading learned during my time at the large Wall Street brokerage firms in the '90s, I also attribute my success in running this proprietary trading business to being extremely responsive and coming up with innovative solutions in a rapidly changing interest rate market. In assessing my role as the trading manager, I am essentially running a service business that requires creative solutions by either learning new software and new products or hiring experts when the task at hand is beyond my capability.

As our trading firm leader, I have successfully navigated several financial crises that created excessive volatility in our markets. I have also navigated several bankruptcies of our clearing houses (i.e. the firms that settle and clear our trades in the marketplace). Trying to always research and learn, adapt and overcome, and have fun in the process, I have led our trading firm to 20 years of success.

Friends of mine whom I have discussed the attributes of an ideal business always ask me, "What is your perfect business?" So, after I assessed my experience and my age, an ideal future business *for me* has the following attributes:

1) Low fixed overhead:
    No long-term retail rent, equipment leases, inventory
2) Low or no accounts receivables:
    Product or service is paid in full at the time of sale
3) Professional employees:
    Low reliance on high-turnover, employee-based businesses
4) No family partners:
    Better to not partner with family or borrow their capital
5) High growth & new industry:
    Exciting to be in an innovative, expanding industry
6) High margin/high turnover:
    Product or service that makes a lot of money frequently
7) Non-luxury product or service:
    Necessary product or maintenance-based
8) Business hours:
    Work when others are working, no weekends/nights
9) Scalable business model:
    Not solely reliant on owner skills to operate and grow
10) Recurring income:
    Minimize the sales/marketing effort to obtain new customers

When I think about a business in terms of fit for a new entrepreneur, I cannot stress enough the concept of keeping it simple and focused on the primary attributes that will make it successful. Many entrepreneurs want to help people who are less fortunate than them by donating products or part of their sales to charity. They may want to help the environment by starting with green initiatives, thereby making their products or services more costly. These are noble efforts and should be thought about, but should not be the focus of a new venture. As a new business owner, you can be compassionate in your hiring, donations, and environmental concerns, but if these efforts cause your business to fail, then what have you achieved? As Daymond John from Shark Tank once said, "Make it, master it, then matter." When running a fledgling start-up, the main focus is the business. You need to succeed to help yourself and your family, and then you can help others.

"Cause life is a lesson; you learn it when you're through."
– Limp Bizkit

www.ingramcontent.com/pod-product-compliance
Lightning Source LLC
Chambersburg PA
CBHW050312230526
45471CB00005B/2138